our WORLD in NUMBERS

DINOSAURS
& OTHER PREHISTORIC LIFE
AN ENCYCLOPEDIA OF FANTASTIC FACTS

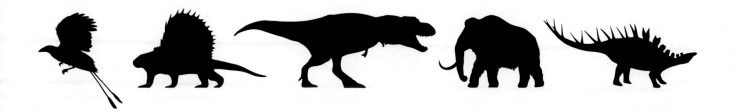

DK

OUR WORLD in NUMBERS

DINOSAURS

& OTHER PREHISTORIC LIFE

AN ENCYCLOPEDIA OF FANTASTIC FACTS

Written by
**WILLIAM POTTER, ALICIA WILLIAMSON,
AND RICHARD MEAD**

Expert consultant
DR. DEAN LOMAX

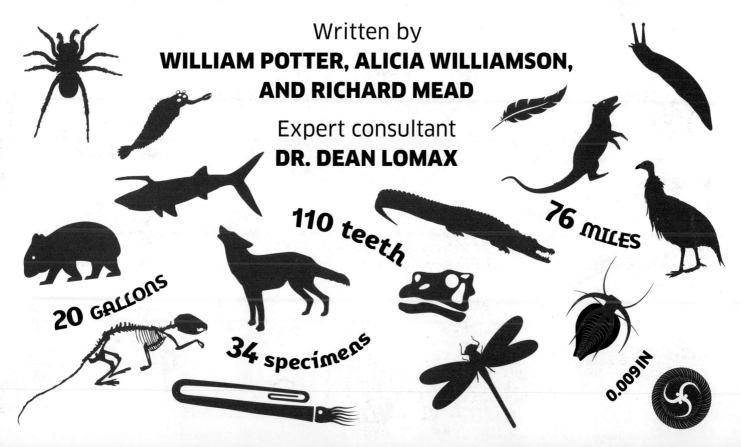

CONTENTS

Penguin
Random
House

Produced for DK by
Dynamo Limited
1 Cathedral Court, Southernhay East, Exeter EX1 1AF

Editorial Partner Alicia Williamson
Design Partner Jeremy Marshall
Expert Consultant Dr. Dean Lomax

Project Editors Sarah Carpenter, Jolyon Goddard
US Editor Mika Jin
US Executive Editor Lori Hand
Senior Art Editor Jacqui Swan
Managing Editor Rachel Fox
Managing Art Editor Owen Peyton Jones
Production Editor Robert Dunn
Production Controller Laura Brand
Jacket Designer Vidushi Chaudhry
DTP Designer Rakesh Kumar
Senior Jackets Coordinator Priyanka Sharma Saddi
Design Development Manager Sophia MTT
Publisher Andrew Mcintyre
Art Director Karen Self
Associate Publishing Director Liz Wheeler
Publishing Director Jonathan Metcalf

First American Edition, 2024
Published in the United States by DK Publishing,
a division of Penguin Random House LLC
1745 Broadway, 20th Floor, New York, NY 10019

Copyright © 2024 Dorling Kindersley Limited
24 25 26 27 28 10 9 8 7 6 5 4 3 2
006–339263–Aug/2024

A catalog record for this book
is available from the Library of Congress.
ISBN 978-0-7440-9878-5

DK books are available at special discounts when
purchased in bulk for sales promotions, premiums,
fund-raising, or educational use.
For details, contact: DK Publishing Special Markets,
1745 Broadway, 20th Floor, New York, NY 10019
SpecialSales@dk.com

Printed and bound in China

www.dk.com

MIX
Paper | Supporting
responsible forestry
FSC™ C018179

This book was made with Forest
Stewardship Council™ certified
paper – one small step in DK's
commitment to a sustainable future.
Learn more at www.dk.com/uk/
information/sustainability

JURASSIC

CRETACEOUS

AFTER THE DINOSAURS

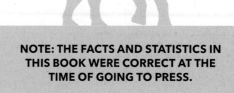

NOTE: THE FACTS AND STATISTICS IN THIS BOOK WERE CORRECT AT THE TIME OF GOING TO PRESS.

DINOSAURS BY THE NUMBERS

We use numbers to count, calculate, measure, and compare. Numbers help us understand our present world—and its 4.5-billion-year past. But how do we get stats about animals that lived and went extinct millions of years ago? Paleontologists (scientists who study ancient life) work with fossils to help us understand prehistoric animals. With 50 new species of dinosaur being discovered each year, the science of fossils is constantly evolving.

What is a fossil?

Fossils are the preserved remains or traces of ancient life. They form when an animal happens to be buried soon after it dies. Either an impression or cast is captured in rock, or an animal's bones are slowly replaced by minerals that turn into rock.

Hidden clues

Besides telling us about an animal's skeleton, fossils contain clues about what they ate, where they lived, how they moved, and more. A skull, for instance, can reveal information about a creature's brain, hearing, sight, sense of smell, and feeding habits.

Our changing understanding

New finds often disprove old ideas about dinosaurs. When the first *Spinosaurus* bones were found in 1912, scientists assumed that this Cretaceous predator had a skull, posture, and tail much like *T. rex*. A more-complete skeleton unearthed in the 2010s has shown that *Spinosaurus* was stranger than we ever imagined. As in the picture below, it had a long thin snout, a much less upright posture, and a powerful, finlike tail to match its tall back sail. These unexpected traits made scientists realize that *Spinosaurus* likely spent a lot of time in water, prowling the depths for prey.

Missing pieces

Fossils only represent a tiny trace of all the life that has existed. Fossilization is a rare, chance event, and some creatures—and parts of creatures—are more likely to be preserved than others. In general, specimens are incomplete, and the hardest parts of them, such as teeth, are most likely to be preserved.

Probably, NOT definitely

Most numbers related to prehistoric creatures come with a "probably," "possibly," "likely," or "maybe." While all the facts in this book are based on scientific studies, the ways that experts come up with stats are constantly being debated and updated. As the evidence, tools, and methods used to make calculations change, the numbers may change, too.

Behind the stats

How do scientists use fossil evidence to make calculations about prehistoric creatures? When something cannot be simply counted or measured, experts create estimates using physical, mathematical, and computer models that draw upon what we know about related species and modern animals with similar features.

How LONG AGO did *Parasaurolophus* live?

Scientists estimate how old a fossil is according to its location within the layers of rock where it was found. Generally, the lower a fossil appears, the older it is. The layers are often dated by measuring radioactive elements within them.

How BIG was the largest sauropod?

A dino's length is measured from the tip of its nose to the end of its often very long tail. Even if scientists have only found a few bones from a particular dinosaur, they can still predict how long it might have been by comparing the bones to those of related species with more complete fossil skeletons. For creatures like a croc, they can also draw on their living relatives with similar body types.

How FAST could *Allosaurus* run?

One way of working out a dinosaur's speed is by measuring the depth of and distance between footprints in its fossil trackways. Hip height and stride length are also important. Alternatively, scientists can estimate how fast a creature was by using the recorded speeds of living animals with similar anatomies.

How STRONG was *Kronosaurus's* bite?

Paleontologists can determine how strong an animal's bite was by reconstructing its jaw muscles and comparing them to those of living animals using computer simulations. The force (strength) of an animal's bite is usually measured in newtons.

How MUCH did the smallest dinosaur weigh?

A dinosaur's mass is often figured out by calculating how much weight its leg bones could hold, using living animals for reference. Today, laser scans of fossil skeletons allow scientists to create computer models of a dino's build that even account for the denseness of different body parts.

TIMELINE OF LIFE

To help make sense of the hundreds of millions of years that comprise Earth's history, scientists have divided it up into different eras, which are further divided into periods.

PRECAMBRIAN ERA

PRECAMBRIAN
4.6 billion years ago–541 MYA
Earth formed when a cloud of gas and dust joined together due to the force of gravity. The first form of life, single-celled organisms, appeared on it 3.5 billion years ago.

PALEOZOIC ERA

CAMBRIAN
541–485 MYA
Multicelled organisms began appearing in the ocean, leading to an "explosion" of invertebrates (animals without backbones).

ORDOVICIAN
485–444 MYA
Ocean-living life continued to flourish and evolve with diverse marine invertebrates, including trilobites and brachiopods.

MESOZOIC ERA

PERMIAN
299–252 MYA
Reptiles, along with mammal ancestors, were already on the rise when a devastating extinction wiped out most life on Earth.

TRIASSIC
252–201 MYA
Recovery from Earth's worst extinction was slow. After millions of years, new animals and the first ever dinosaurs, pterosaurs, and ichthyosaurs appeared.

CENOZOIC ERA

PALEOGENE
66–23 MYA
With dinosaurs long gone, mammals had the chance to take over and thrive. They became more diverse and much larger on land and in the sea, too.

NEOGENE
23–2.6 MYA
Many animals that still exist today appeared during this period, including elephants and apes. It was also when early human ancestors began to walk upright.

Note: MYA means "million years ago."

SILURIAN
444–419 MYA

Many plants thrived in the sea while others lacking leaves, flowers, or roots spread on land. Coral reefs began to grow in warm oceans.

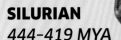

DEVONIAN
419–359 MYA

Sometimes known as the "Age of Fishes" due to the abundance of sea life, the Devonian saw some fish leave the water to become the first amphibians on land.

CARBONIFEROUS
359–299 MYA

Extensive swampy forests formed on land, giving rise to enormous plant-eating bugs. The very first reptiles appeared and were tiny by comparison.

JURASSIC
201–145 MYA

By now Earth was taken over with dinosaurs of all kinds, from enormous, lumbering plant-eaters to quick, meat-eating predators, and the first birds.

CRETACEOUS
145–66 MYA

Flowering plants spread everywhere as dinosaurs dominated the entire planet... until an asteroid (space rock) hit Earth, causing almost all the dinosaurs to die out.

QUATERNARY
2.6 MYA–today

There have been many ice ages during this period. Fearsome megafauna went extinct toward the end of the last one. As early as 300,000 years ago, modern humans appeared in Africa and then across the globe.

THE FOSSIL RECORD

Earth is covered with strata (layers of rock) that have built up over millions of years. Each layer represents a specific period in Earth's history. The plant and animal fossils that appear in these layers help show what life was like during the corresponding periods.

BEFORE THE DINOSAURS

The FIRST ANIMALS

Perhaps as much as 800 million years ago, the very first animals evolved in the sea. These were simple creatures, with saclike bodies and no skeletons of any kind. They were followed by mysterious animals that resembled leaves, feathers, or flat, quilted worms.

Dickinsonia

looked like a flat, oval **WORM WITH NO HEAD** and was first discovered in **1946** in **AUSTRALIA.** It lived around **570 MILLION YEARS AGO.**

TRIBRACHIDIUM HERALDICUM was a **DISC-SHAPED CREATURE**

up to **1³/₅IN** (4cm) in diameter. It lived on the **SEAFLOOR** and had

3 arms sprouting from its center.

DICKINSONIA

ranged in size from the

1/₅IN- (4mm-) long **DICKINSONIA COSTATA** to the rug-sized **DICKINSONIA REX** at

3FT 3IN (1m).

Spriggina

was a **TINY CREATURE** with **40 segments** that lived in shallow, sandy waters in the **LATE PRECAMBRIAN PERIOD.**

More than **1,000** fossilized specimens of the **OVAL, SLUGLIKE** *KIMBERELLA* have been found in **NORTHWEST RUSSIA.**

Mawsonites spriggi is a circular Ediacaran fossil, with **19 radiations** coming from the center, and it is a **COMPLETE MYSTERY.**

Scientists thought *DICKINSONIA* might be a **FUNGUS,** until a **MOLECULAR TEST** showed that **93%** of it was **MADE OF FAT,** proving it was **AN ANIMAL.**

Fossils of **MARINE ANIMAL** *Swartpuntia* show it had up to **6 FEATHERLIKE SHEETS** of **THIN TUBES SPROUTING** from **A STEM.**

The **FIRST FOSSIL** of the **PRECAMBRIAN** leaflike animal *Charnia masoni* was discovered by **15-YEAR-OLD** schoolchildren in **LEICESTERSHIRE, UK,** in the **1950s.**

Dickinsonia's body had **12–74** pairs of **MATCHING SEGMENTS.**

IN 2010, in Newfoundland, Canada, **70** **fossilized animal trails** were found. The **EARLIEST EVER DISCOVERED,** they were left by **CREATURES LIKE SEA ANEMONES** from **565 MILLION YEARS AGO.**

The **EARLIEST-KNOWN ANIMAL PREDATOR** is *AURORALUMINA ATTENBOROUGHII,* a **560-MILLION-YEAR-OLD JELLYFISH RELATIVE.** This **8IN-** (20cm-) tall creature **LOOKED LIKE A LANTERN** with food-grabbing **TENTACLES.**

Wiwaxia looked a bit like an **ARMORED PORCUPINE**—it **DIDN'T** have a **DISTINCT HEAD** but did have

2 or 3 rows

of **SHARP TEETH.**

The **EARLIEST-KNOWN VERTEBRATES** were a pair of

518-million-year-old

fossilized **FISHLIKE CREATURES** called **HAIKOUICHTHYS,** named in **1999.**

Some scientists think the **RAPID EXPANSION** of **NEW LIFE FORMS** during the **CAMBRIAN EXPLOSION** lasted for

20 million years.

Archaeocyathids, which **FIRST APPEARED** around

525 million years ago,

were among the **EARLIEST SPONGES.**

Anomalocaris was the **TOP PREDATOR** in Cambrian seas, capturing prey

with **2 spiky claws** on its head.

OPABINIA'S body had

16 segments,

with **OVERLAPPING FLAPS** on each side—it **MIGHT** have **MOVED THESE** like a **WAVE** to **PROPEL** itself through the water.

Hallucigenia had

7 PAIRS

OF STIFF SPINES on its body and a **BLOB ON ONE END** that took more than **50 YEARS** for scientists to officially **IDENTIFY AS ITS HEAD.**

The **1⅕IN–** (3cm-) wide **Echmatocrinus** had a **CONE-SHAPED BODY** underneath a ring of **7–9 TENTACLES.**

The **Burgess Shale** site in **CANADA** is a treasure trove of **CAMBRIAN PERIOD** fossils—more than

65,000

have been found there.

The CAMBRIAN EXPLOSION

About 530 million years ago, land on Earth was barren. However, during the Cambrian explosion, an amazing array of new animals began appearing in the seas. Unlike the soft-bodied creatures that lived before them, the fascinating new arrivals had hard shells, spikes, and external skeletons.

The small, shrimplike **MARRELLA** had at least **50 feathery legs,** which it **BEAT** to **SWIM** and used as **GILLS** for **BREATHING UNDERWATER.**

MOST of the **FOSSILS** from the **CAMBRIAN EXPLOSION** have been found in **2 PLACES—CANADA** and **CHINA.**

The bizarre-looking *Opabinia* had **5 EYES** atop stalks on its head.

Around **1,500** fossils of *OTTOIA* have been found— **ANALYSIS** of **DIGESTED FOOD** shows that it was a **CANNIBAL.**

MARRELLA'S head was covered by a **PROTECTIVE SHIELD** with **4 long spikes,** which may have been **IRIDESCENT.**

Fascinating TRILOBITES

The seas of the Paleozoic Era were teeming with trilobites. Many foraged for food on the seabed, although some could swim. They had external skeletons, which they shed and replaced as they grew. Most trilobite fossils are of these discarded exoskeletons, rather than the whole animal.

The **EARLIEST TRILOBITES** that have been found are **520–530 million years old,** from countries including Morocco, Spain, and Russia.

Some **TRILOBITES** had **2 digestive tracts** connected to their stomach, **INSTEAD OF 1.**

They are **EXTINCT NOW,** but trilobites lived on Earth for more than **270 million years.** That's **50,000 TIMES LONGER THAN MODERN HUMANS** have existed.

The **LARGEST TRILOBITE FOSSIL,** *Isotelus rex,* was discovered in Manitoba, Canada, and is an amazing **28IN** (71cm) long.

The **"TRI"** at the start of a **TRILOBITE'S NAME** means **3** and refers to how the main part of the creature's **EXOSKELETON** is **DIVIDED** into **3 lobes** (parts).

The **SMALLEST** trilobites, such as *CTENOPYGE CECILIAE*, were **LESS THAN** **1/10IN** (3mm) long.

Like **MODERN INSECTS**, most **TRILOBITES** had **2 compound eyes** with lots of lenses. However, some trilobites, such as the mud-dwelling **TRINUCLEUS**, **DIDN'T HAVE ANY EYES** at all.

In **2023**, a **3-D SCAN** of a **465-MILLION-YEAR-OLD** trilobite, *BOHEMOLICHAS INCOLA*, revealed the shell fragments of **ECHINODERMS** it had **EATEN BEFORE DEATH**.

Experts have **IDENTIFIED** more than **22,000 SPECIES** of **trilobites** so far.

In addition to having 3 lobes, a trilobite's body was divided into **3 SEGMENTS:** the **CEPHALON** (its head), **THORAX** (its body), and **PYGIDIUM** (its tail).

In **1886**, archaeologists investigating a **15,000-YEAR-OLD** French prehistoric cave site found a **400-million-year-old trilobite** that had been turned into a **PENDANT** by **DRILLING A HOLE** in its **TAIL**.

Walliserops had a **3-pronged spear** appendage on its head, which might have been **USED FOR FIGHTING**.

Spiny ECHINODERMS

These simple marine invertebrates have spines or bumps on their tough outer surfaces and often look like stars. Echinoderms have been living on the seafloor for hundreds of millions of years and many, such as brittle stars, crinoids, and sea urchins, are still around today.

The **EARLIEST-KNOWN ECHINODERM** may be **ARKARUA ADAMI**, found in Australia and dating to around **555 MILLION YEARS AGO.**

Brittle stars such as **Palaeocoma** had **5 LONG ARMS**, and **5 TOOTHED JAWS** in a **STAR-SHAPED MOUTH**, which was also the **ECHINODERM'S BOTTOM.**

Encrinus, a type of **CRINOID** called a **SEA LILY**, could grow to over **3FT** (1m) tall and had a ring of **10 FEATHERY ARMS** at the top of a stalk that were used to catch food.

A fossil of a **430-million-year-old echinoderm** found in **2017** was the **FIRST EXAMPLE** discovered with preserved **TUBE FEET,** used for feeding and moving.

Instead of sticking to the seafloor, giant **Seirocrinus** could grow together in **MASSIVE FLOATING COLONIES**. One fossil shows **HUNDREDS OF SPECIMENS**, up to **65FT** (20m) tall, attached to the underside of a **39FT-** (12m-) long **TREE TRUNK.**

In **2021, 2 AMATEUR PALEONTOLOGISTS** discovered a **fossil site in England** that contained more than **1,000 ECHINODERM SPECIMENS,** including **BRITTLE STARS** and **SEA LILIES.**

More than **7,000** species of **ECHINODERMS** live in **OCEANS** around the world **TODAY**, but more than **13,000 SPECIES** are known to be **EXTINCT.**

Little **Hemicidaris** had savage **3¼IN-** (8cm-) long **SPINES** around its **SMALL BODY** that increased its diameter from **1½IN** (4cm) to **8IN** (20cm).

Modern **ECHINODERMS** have **5-fold SYMMETRY,** but some ancient species were **ASYMMETRICAL.**

An **ECHINODERM** can have **100s** of feeding arms but **NO HEAD** or **BRAIN.**

At least 6,000 **SPECIES** of fossil **CRINOIDS** have been **IDENTIFIED.**

Crinoids had up to **200** feeding arms in **MULTIPLES OF 5.**

Fuxianhuia

had a **SHELL COVERING ITS HEAD** with **2 stalked eyes** and **2 antennae.**

About
50%
of the **FOSSILS FOUND** in **CHENGJIANG** are those of **ARTHROPODS.**

Arthropods
make up more than
85%
of all **LIVING SPECIES TODAY.**

Beside one **FOSSILIZED ADULT** found in **2018** were

4
Fuxianhuia babies,
possibly the **WORLD'S OLDEST EXAMPLE OF PARENTING!**

FUXIANHUIA

This extinct marine arthropod from the Cambrian is the unofficial mascot for one of the world's most important fossil sites: China's Chengjiang Biota. *Fuxianhuia* specimens found here are so well preserved, they include details of its heart, brain, and guts that show just how complex life already was more than 500 million years ago.

The *Fuxianhuia* remains include the **EARLIEST EXAMPLE** of a **FOSSILIZED BRAIN** in **3 PARTS** like that of modern insects.

Among the **EARLIEST ARTHROPODS,** *Fuxianhuia* has been dated to a staggering **520 MILLION YEARS AGO.**

The **SHRIMPLIKE FUXIANHUIA** was only about **3IN** (7.6cm) long. The **BIGGEST FOUND** is **4⅓IN** (11cm).

CHENGJIANG was discovered by **PALEONTOLOGIST HOU XIAN-GUANG** in **1984** and designated as an **UNESCO WORLD HERITAGE SITE 28 years later.**

Famous for the surprising preservation of ancient, **SOFT-BODIED CREATURES, CHENGJIANG** has yielded more than **250 SPECIES** of **PLANTS AND ANIMALS.**

Hou named *Fuxianhuia protensa* in **1987; 100s OF SPECIMENS** have been found in mudstone since.

FUXIANHUIA had **35–45** pairs of **TINY 2-BRANCHED LEGS.**

A specimen uncovered in **2014** included the **EARLIEST-KNOWN CARDIOVASCULAR SYSTEM,** with a **SIMPLE TUBULAR HEART** spanning **7 segments** of its body.

Fuxianhuia had a **SEGMENTED BODY** with about **31 SECTIONS,** including **14 ON ITS TAIL.**

Awesome AMMONOIDS

Like today's octopuses and squid, ammonites and other ammonoids were cephalopods. These soft-bodied creatures lived in the ocean from the Devonian to just beyond the Cretaceous Period. Most of them had ornate, coiled shells with chambers that could hold air to help them float. The majority of ammonoid fossils are just these shells.

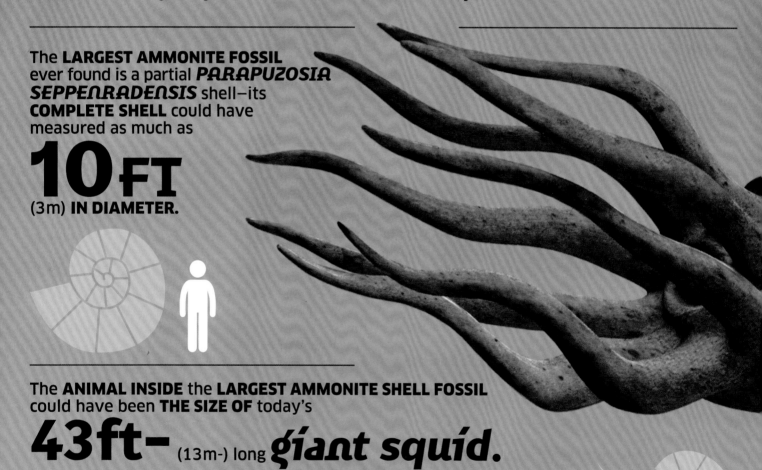

The **LARGEST AMMONITE FOSSIL** ever found is a partial *PARAPUZOSIA SEPPENRADENSIS* shell—its **COMPLETE SHELL** could have measured as much as

10 FT
(3m) **IN DIAMETER.**

The **ANIMAL INSIDE** the **LARGEST AMMONITE SHELL FOSSIL** could have been **THE SIZE OF** today's

43ft- (13m-) long *giant squid.*

Like many of their **CLOSEST LIVING RELATIVES** (coleoids such as squid), **AMMONOIDS** probably had

10 TENTACLES.

An **AMMONITE SHELL** had

2 main parts:
the **PHRAGMOCONE,** a series of internal chambers that **FILLED WITH GAS** to keep it buoyant, and the **BODY CHAMBER** where the animal **LIVED.**

Some **FEMALE AMMONITES** were up to

4 times
larger than the **MALES.**

SCIENTISTS HAVE IDENTIFIED more than **10,000 SPECIES** of **ammonites.**

AMMONOIDS first **APPEARED ON EARTH** around **416 million YEARS AGO.**

AMMONOIDS survived

3
MAJOR EXTINCTION EVENTS, including one in the **LATE PERMIAN** that **WIPED OUT 96%** of **ALL MARINE SPECIES.**

AMMONOIDS POPULATED the **OCEANS** for around

350 MILLION YEARS.

The **SMALLEST-KNOWN AMMONOID** is the *MAXIMITES* species. Its shell grew to just $^2/_5$**IN** (1cm) in **DIAMETER,** the size of a **SMALL FINGERNAIL.**

Like **MODERN-DAY CEPHALOPODS,** some **AMMONITES** are likely to have lived in water up to a **MAXIMUM DEPTH** of **820FT** (250m).

Some **AMMONOIDS,** called *HETEROMORPHS,* had **UNCOILED SHELLS.** A fossil of *Diplomoceras maximum* shows it had a **PAPERCLIP-SHAPED SHELL** **13FT** (4m) **LONG** if straightened.

In the **7th** century CE, **AMMONITES** were **MISTAKEN** for **PETRIFIED SNAKES** and sold with **SNAKE HEADS** carved into them.

IDMONARACHNE BRASIERI, an "almost spider" from

305 million years ago,

could probably **PRODUCE SILK** but did **NOT YET HAVE SPINNERETS** to spin it into webs.

Palaeoisopus problematicus

was a large **SEA SPIDER** from the Devonian Period with **LEGS SPANNING**

12½IN (32cm),

as **WIDE AS A LARGE PIZZA.**

99 million years ago,

ticks fed on dinosaurs. One **PREHISTORIC BLOODSUCKER, DEINOCROTON DRACULI,** has been **DISCOVERED** in **AMBER** next to a dinosaur feather.

In **2018,** the remains of

Chimerarachne yingi

were discovered in amber. The

⅓IN- (7.5mm-) long

arachnid had **FANGS** and a **WHIPLIKE TAIL.**

The giant **"SEA SCORPION"** Pterygotus grew to be as much as **5ft 9in** (1.75m) long.

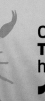

One of the **FIRST ANIMALS TO WALK ON LAND** may have been the

1¾IN- (4.5cm-) long prehistoric scorpion

PARIOSCORPIO VENATOR.

The **LARGEST-EVER MARINE ARTHROPOD** was the **400-MILLION-YEAR-OLD** eurypterid or "sea scorpion,"

Jaekelopterus rhenaniae.

At **8FT** (2.5m) long, it was as **BIG AS A DOOR.**

CHELICERATES

First appearing in the sea 510 million years ago, chelicerates were animals with a segmented body and clawlike front limbs (but no antennae). Prehistoric examples include early arachnids–spiders, scorpions, ticks, and mites–plus horseshoe crabs, sea spiders, and giant sea scorpions.

Triasacarus fedelei, a **TRIASSIC GALL MITE** just **0.008IN** (0.21mm) long, was **FOUND IN AMBER** in Italy.

ONE OF THE LARGEST SCORPIONS of all time was *PULMONOSCORPIUS KIRKTONENSIS.* Found in Scotland, this **28IN-** (70cm-) long giant lived around **340 MILLION YEARS** ago.

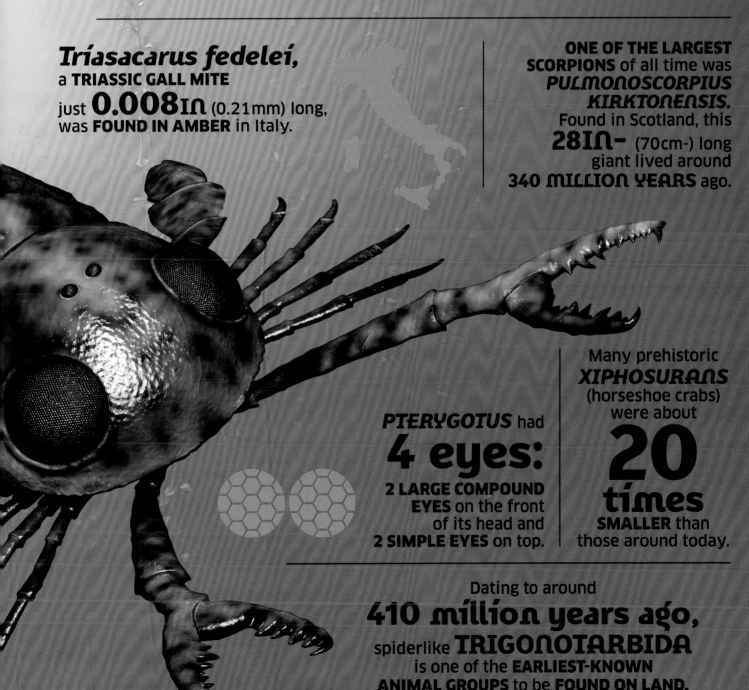

PTERYGOTUS had **4 eyes:** **2 LARGE COMPOUND EYES** on the front of its head and **2 SIMPLE EYES** on top.

Many prehistoric *XIPHOSURANS* (horseshoe crabs) were about **20 times SMALLER** than those around today.

Dating to around **410 million years ago,** spiderlike **TRIGONOTARBIDA** is one of the **EARLIEST-KNOWN ANIMAL GROUPS** to be **FOUND ON LAND.**

Insects and
MYRIAPODS

These two groups are types of arthropod—segmented animals with exoskeletons (tough outer coverings) and no backbones. They were the first creatures to step onto land over 400 million years ago. While many resembled modern-day bugs, some grew much bigger, especially in tropical forests of the Carboniferous.

The **LARGEST LAND-BASED INVERTEBRATE** of all time was the **GIANT MILLIPEDE** *ARTHROPLEURA ARMATA.* It grew up to **8FT 6IN** (2.6m), longer than a **RATTLESNAKE.**

The **FIRST EVIDENCE** of **CENTIPEDES** dates to **428 million years ago,** from **REMAINS** found in **SCOTLAND, UK.**

The earliest named example of a **LEPIDOPTERAN** (butterfly or moth) is *Archaeolepis mane,* an Early Jurassic moth identified by a single **1/5IN-** (5mm-) **LONG WING** captured in mudstone.

The **OLDEST-KNOWN INSECT FOSSIL** dates to **410 million years ago.** *RHYNIOGNATHA HIRSTI* was found in **SCOTLAND.**

Grasshoppers
evolved during the **TRIASSIC PERIOD,** nearly **200 MILLION YEARS BEFORE GRASS APPEARED!**

DISEASE-CARRYING MOSQUITOES may have been bothering dinosaurs **100 MILLION YEARS AGO.** *Priscoculex burmanicus* was found fossilized in **MID-CRETACEOUS AMBER.**

Some of the **EARLIEST** examples of **ants** were found **PRESERVED IN CRETACEOUS AMBER** from **BURMA** (Myanmar). In one fossil dating to **99 MILLION YEARS AGO,** **2 SPECIES OF ANT** are **FIGHTING** one another!

CARBONIFEROUS INSECTS likely grew to **GIANT SIZES** due to **OXYGEN LEVELS** in the atmosphere being **UP TO 10% HIGHER** than the **21%** oxygen in **TODAY'S AIR.**

The **LARGEST-EVER INSECT** was the Carboniferous dragonfly relative *MEGANEURA MONYI,* which had a **WINGSPAN** up to **30IN** (75cm) across, the same as a **SPARROWHAWK.**

LITTLE IS KNOWN about what **ARTHROPLEURA** ate because **zero MOUTHPARTS** have ever been found in the **FOSSIL RECORD.**

ARTHROPLEURA had up to **64 LEGS.** Today's millipedes have up to **1,300.**

Fantastic
JAWLESS FISH

The first fish, which appeared during the Cambrian Period more than 500 million years ago, had no jaws. They sucked in and filtered food from the seabed, and some developed bony or spiky plates for protection. Two groups of eel-like jawless fish survive to this day, hagfish and lampreys.

Haikouichthys

was a **PRIMITIVE JAWLESS FISH** that lived **518 MILLION YEARS AGO.**

The ancient **HAIKOUICHTHYS** had the **BEGINNINGS** of a **BACKBONE** and was just

1IN (2.5cm) long, the length of a **TADPOLE.**

ATELEASPIS had a **MOUTH** and

10 pairs of **GILLS** on its **UNDERSIDE,** suggesting it **FED FROM** the **SEABED.**

The **8-gilled**
ASTRASPIS
gets its **NAME**, meaning
"**STAR SHIELD,**" from the
STAR-SHAPED NODULES
that **COVERED**
ITS BODY.

Ateleaspis
was the **FIRST-KNOWN FISH** with
2 PAIRED
PECTORAL FINS.

There is only **1** confirmed species of **CEPHALASPIS, C. LYELLI**, first described in **1835.**

Around **30**
million years
before **JAWS EVOLVED,**
Loganellia
developed some of the first
TOOTHLIKE STRUCTURES
in its **THROAT.**

Cephalaspis,
meaning "**HEAD SHIELD,**"
was a **TROUT-SIZED**
PRIMITIVE FISH, up to
12 IN (30cm) long,
with **HOOF-SHAPED BONY**
ARMOR over its head.

LOGANELLIA
was a **THELODONT**
(a jawless fish
without armor)
COVERED with up to
20,000
DENTICLES
(toothlike scales).

Sacabambaspis
had a **BODY LENGTH** of up to
14 IN
(35cm) and a large **HEAD**
SHIELD that included
20 SMALL PLATES
on each side
with **GILLS HIDDEN**
BEHIND them.

Though it had **NO JAWS,**
SACABAMBASPIS
had a **MOUTH LINED** with about
60 bony plates
it could use to **GATHER FOOD.**

The **EARLIEST**
LAMPREY FOSSILS
date to **360**
MILLION YEARS AGO
and look the same as
modern lampreys.

Parameteoraspis
had a horseshoe-shaped
HEAD SHIELD
that was
16 IN
(40cm) wide.

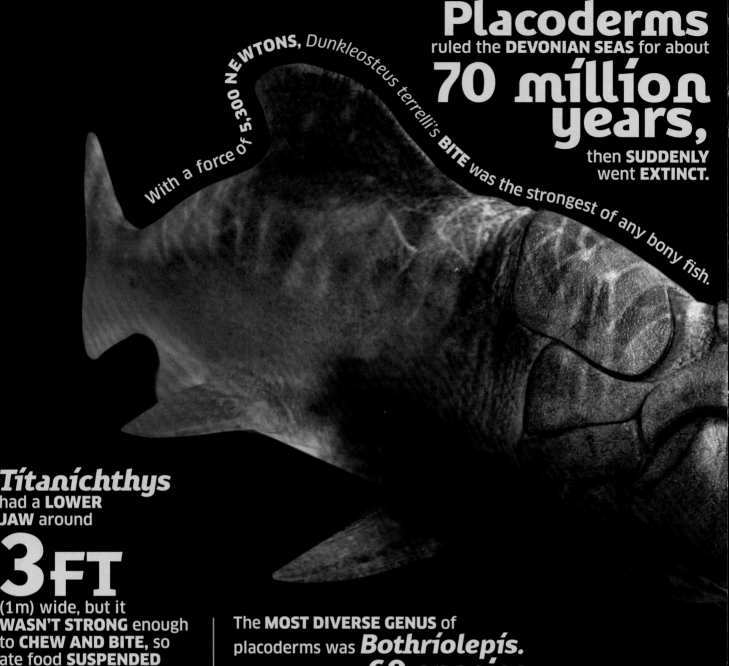

With a force of **5,300 NEWTONS,** Dunkleosteus terrelli's **BITE** was the strongest of any bony fish.

Placoderms
ruled the **DEVONIAN SEAS** for about
70 million years,
then **SUDDENLY** went **EXTINCT.**

Titanichthys
had a **LOWER JAW** around
3 FT
(1m) wide, but it **WASN'T STRONG** enough to **CHEW AND BITE,** so ate food **SUSPENDED IN THE WATER** instead.

The **MOST DIVERSE GENUS of** placoderms was *Bothriolepis.* It contained over **60 species.**

The **12 IN-** (30cm-) long *ROLFOSTEUS* had a **HORNLIKE SNOUT** that might have been used for **UNCOVERING PREY HIDING IN THE SEABED.**

Placoderms
had **2 PAIRS OF MUSCLES**
linking the top of the head to the shoulder bones **INSTEAD OF 1 PAIR,** allowing for a **QUICK BITING ACTION.**

Astonishing ARMORED FISH

Also called placoderms, armored fish were among the first fish to develop biting jaws, with bony plates as teeth. They were also the first to grow to huge sizes. Most had hinged shields of bone over their heads and the tops of their bodies.

Placoderms were the **first** **ANIMALS TO HAVE ABS** (abdominal muscles).

A **380-MILLION-YEAR-OLD** fossil of a *Materpiscis attenboroughi* captures the **EARLIEST-KNOWN LIVE BIRTH.**

Estimates for the length of the **LARGEST PLACODERM,** *DUNKLEOSTEUS TERRELLI,* range from **15FT** (4.5m) to **33FT** (10m).

The **SHIELD OF BONE** on the **HEAD** of *Dunkleosteus* was **2IN** (5cm) thick.

Dunkleosteus weighed around **2 TONS,** the same as a great white shark.

The **oldest 3-D fossilized heart** discovered has **2 chambers.** It was in a *MCNAMARASPIS KAPRIOS* found in **2022** in Australia's Devonian **GOGO REEF FORMATION.**

Gemuendina was typically **12IN** (30cm) long. **UNLIKE OTHER ARMORED FISH,** it had **STAR-SHAPED SCALES** in its mouth to grasp prey, rather than **PLATES OF BONE.**

Sensational
SHARKS

Sharks and chimeras (ghost sharks) are cartilaginous fish, with skeletons made of flexible cartilage. Among the first fish in the sea, sharks and their relatives have been swimming in our oceans for at least 420 million years and include monsters much bigger than today's great whites.

The buzzsaw shark *Helicoprion* had a **CIRCULAR SAWLIKE WHORL** with up to **150 TEETH** sticking out of its lower jaw.

The males of the **6IN-** (15cm-) long *FALCATUS* had a long, swordlike appendage coming out of their heads.

A fossil from **BEAR GULCH** in Montana, dating to **325 million years ago,** shows a female *FALCATUS* gripping a male's head spine with her teeth.

The **LARGEST-KNOWN PREHISTORIC SHARK** was *Otodus megalodon,* which grew to an estimated **59FT** (18m) in length, more than **3 times longer** than a **GREAT WHITE SHARK.**

COW SHARKS have **7 gills** on each side of their heads. Most other sharks **ONLY HAVE 5.** Cow sharks have kept this feature since the **JURASSIC PERIOD.**

HAMMERHEAD SHARKS are the **NEWEST** members of the **SHARK FAMILY,** having evolved only **23 million years ago.**

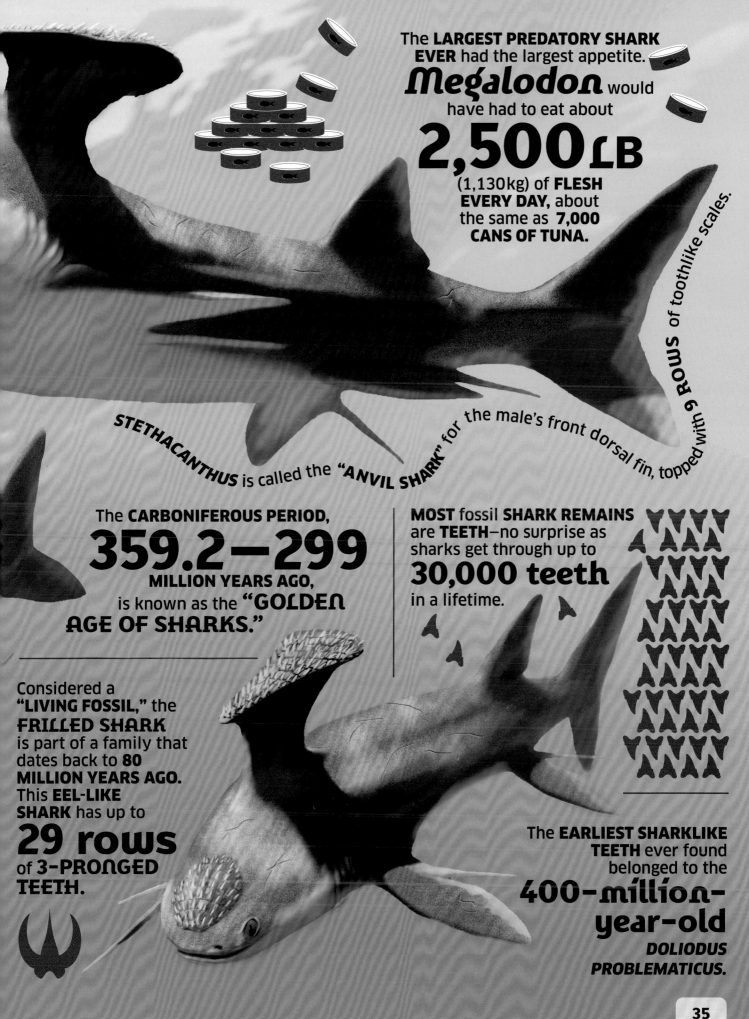

The **LARGEST PREDATORY SHARK EVER** had the largest appetite. **Megalodon** would have had to eat about **2,500 LB** (1,130 kg) of **FLESH EVERY DAY**, about the same as **7,000 CANS OF TUNA**.

STETHACANTHUS is called the **"ANVIL SHARK"** for the male's front dorsal fin, topped with **9 ROWS** of toothlike scales.

The **CARBONIFEROUS PERIOD**, **359.2 – 299 MILLION YEARS AGO**, is known as the **"GOLDEN AGE OF SHARKS."**

MOST fossil **SHARK REMAINS** are **TEETH**—no surprise as sharks get through up to **30,000 teeth** in a lifetime.

Considered a **"LIVING FOSSIL,"** the **FRILLED SHARK** is part of a family that dates back to **80 MILLION YEARS AGO**. This **EEL-LIKE SHARK** has up to **29 rows** of **3-PRONGED TEETH**.

The **EARLIEST SHARKLIKE TEETH** ever found belonged to the **400-million-year-old** *DOLIODUS PROBLEMATICUS*.

TOP 5 OLDEST ANIMALS

These amazing animal groups have survived hundreds of millions of years, even through mass extinctions. They appeared long before the dinosaurs and are still around today.

COMB JELLIES • Ctenophora
Timespan: **C.700 MILLION YEARS**

There is ongoing debate about which was the first true animal, but a 2023 DNA analysis suggests it may well be a relative of the comb jelly. Not to be confused with jellyfish, these gelatinous plankton-eaters use eight rows of hairlike cilia to propel themselves through the water.

2 SPONGES • Porifera
Timespan: **C.600 MILLION YEARS**

Sponges don't have brains, stomachs, or any organs at all, so it makes sense that they might be among the first animals. In 2015, a ½₅in- (1mm-) wide fossil found in China proved to be a primitive sponge dating to 600 million years ago. Today, there are thousands of species of these simple marine invertebrates.

3 JELLYFISH • Cnidaria
Timespan: **MORE THAN 500 MILLION YEARS**

These soft-bodied sea creatures do not fossilize well. Still, there is evidence of them in the fossil record dating back to 508 million years ago—a *Burgessomedusa phasmiformis,* with 90 stubby tentacles, was uncovered in a Canadian mountain. Today, they swim in every ocean on Earth.

4 NAUTILOIDS • Cephalopoda
Timespan: **C.500 MILLION YEARS**

Known for their chambered shells and soft, tentacled bodies, more than 2,500 species of nautiloids have been identified in the fossil record. Only six types of nautilus survive today, in the tropical Pacific—and they're tiny in comparison to their meters-long ancestors.

5 VELVET WORMS • Onychophora
Timespan: **C.500 MILLION YEARS**

These fuzzy, caterpillar-like predators with loads of short, squishy feet have been living on land for around 400 million years—and haven't changed dramatically in that time. But many scientists trace their lineage even further back to strange Cambrian sea creatures such as *Hallucigenia*.

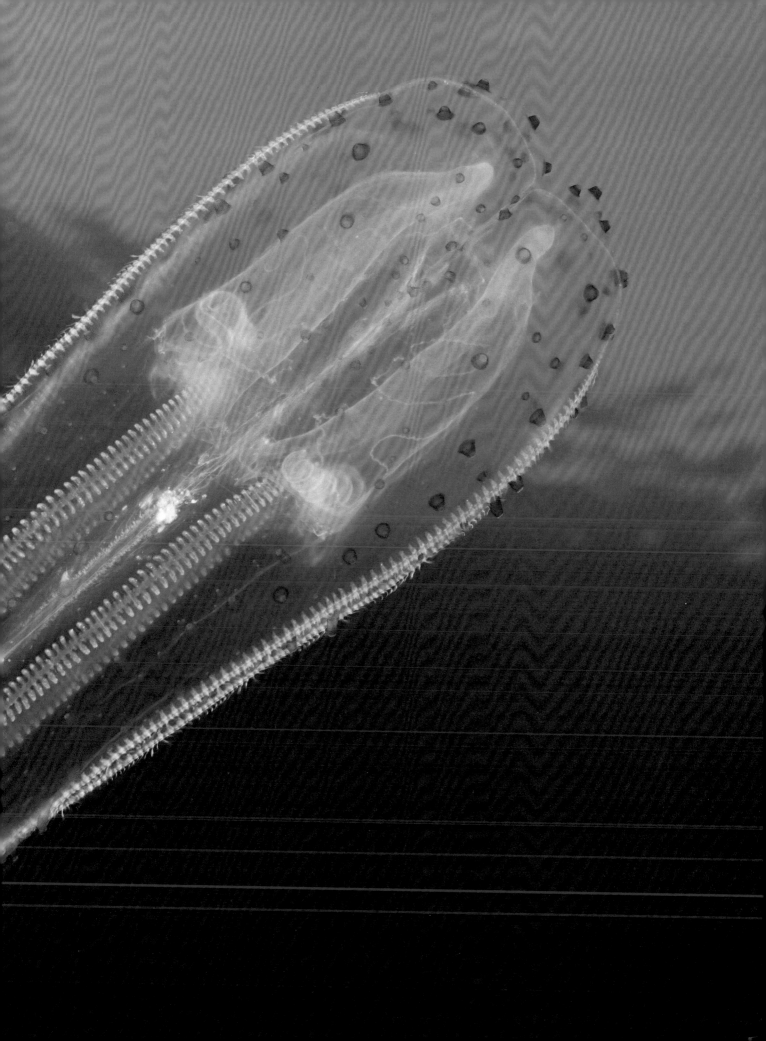

A contender for the **LARGEST LAND ANIMAL** from **295 MILLION YEARS AGO**, *Eryops* grew up to **6FT 6IN** (2m) long, the **SIZE** of an **ALLIGATOR**.

DIPLOCAULUS was first discovered in **1877** in Illinois, in rocks dating to **300 MILLION YEARS AGO**.

The **LARGEST-KNOWN AMPHIBIAN** of all time is thought to be *Prionosuchus plummeri*. This Early Permian, **LONG-SNOUTED CREATURE** is estimated to have reached a length of **30FT** (9m), the same as a *Triceratops*.

ERYOPS'S LARGE FLAT SKULL made up about **1/3** of its **BODY LENGTH**.

9 SETS of **BONES** of the **EARLY AMPHIBIAN** *Seymouria* were discovered in **1882**, but it would be about **50 YEARS** before they were identified.

ERYOPS was a **SQUAT PREDATOR** estimated to have weighed up to **440LB** (200kg).

To **CATCH FISH** and other slippery prey, *ERYOPS* had **3 PAIRS OF CURVED FANGS**, the longest of which were **1IN** (2.5cm).

Amazing
AMPHIBIANS

The first amphibians evolved from fish during the Devonian Period, becoming the first animals with backbones to live on land. To survive out of water, amphibians developed legs, their skin adapted to retain moisture, and their gills were replaced with lungs, but they still returned to water to lay their soft eggs.

One of the earliest-recorded amphibian predecessors, *Ichthyostega* had **7 DIGITS ON ITS HIND FEET.**

An early swamp-dwelling amphibian, *Diplocaulus* was **3FT 3IN** (1m) in length. Its **BOOMERANG-SHAPED SKULL** was up to **13IN** (33cm) wide, which would have made it hard for predators to swallow.

Fossilized *DISCOSAURISCUS* skulls up to **1⅓IN** (32mm) long were found to have **EXTERNAL GILLS.** These are **MISSING ON LARGER SKULLS,** showing their **METAMORPHOSIS** from **TADPOLE TO ADULT.**

One of the **FIRST VERTEBRATES WITH LIMBS,** *Acanthostega* was about **24IN** (60cm) long and had both **GILLS AND LUNGS.**

Acanthostega had **8 digits** on each front **WEBBED FOOT.**

The toothy, **5FT-** (1.5m-) long amphibian ancestor *Crassigyrinus* could have opened its jaws as wide as **60 DEGREES,** about **20°** more than a **HUMAN.**

Impressive
PROTOMAMMALS

The dominant land animals during the Permian Period were protomammals, also known as early synapsids. While many looked like reptiles, they were really ancestors of mammals and mammal-like animals, as revealed by the similar structures of their skulls.

PROTOMAMMALS FIRST APPEAR IN THE FOSSIL RECORD around **310 million years ago,** during the **CARBONIFEROUS PERIOD.**

DIMETRODON was the **LARGEST LAND PREDATOR** the world had seen at that time, growing up to

15FT
(4.6m) **IN LENGTH.**

An adult
Dimetrodon
WEIGHED an estimated
660LB
(300kg), about the **SAME AS A TIGER.**

The **SMALLEST-KNOWN DIMETRODON** is
D. teutonis,
which was **24IN** (60cm) long, the same as a **BEARDED DRAGON,** and weighed about **31LB** (14kg).

CROCODILELIKE
Ophiacodon
had the **LONGEST SKULL** of any early synapsid, measuring up to
20 IN
(50cm) **LONG.**

Dimetrodon had a **TALL SAIL FIN** across its back that could rise up to **5 FT** (1.5m).

The bulky, **PLANT-EATING** *Moschops* had a **SKULL** that was
4½ IN
(11.5cm) **THICK** on top, ideal for **HEADBUTTING.**

Discovered in
1938,
the insect-eating, **IGUANA-SIZED** *MESENOSAURUS* was the **first PROTOMAMMAL** found in **RUSSIA.**

The **FIRST *DIMETRODON* FOSSILS** were discovered in 1845, in a well on a Canadian farm, but the **FIRST *DIMETRODON* TAIL** was not found until **82 years LATER.** It was
5 FT
(1.5m) **LONG.**

There are
14
known species of *Dimetrodon*—
13 from **NORTH AMERICA** and **1** from **GERMANY.**

The small **GOPHERLIKE SYNAPSID**
Diictodon
dug spiral-shaped **BURROWS** up to
29 IN
(75cm) **DEEP.**

Fossil tracks
that were probably made by a **DIMETRODON** have been found in **NEW MEXICO,** showing its
5-toed
FEET in the rock.

LARGE and **FINNED** like *DIMETRODON,* *EDAPHOSAURUS* had up to
150
TEETH but **ATE ONLY PLANTS.**

DIMETRODON lived
40 MILLION
years **BEFORE** the **FIRST DINOSAURS.**

THE GREAT DYING

The worst extinction event in Earth's history occurred at the end of the Permian Period, around 252 million years ago. This catastrophe is known as the "Great Dying," and most animal and plant species were wiped out. It was likely caused by major volcanic activity flooding the atmosphere with carbon dioxide, raising temperatures, and turning the oceans more acidic.

TEMPERATURES WENT UP by about

14°F
(8°C).

Evidence of Late Permian **VOLCANIC ACTIVITY** can be found in **SIBERIA** where there is a **3 MILLION SQ MILE** (7 million sq km) layer of ancient lava underground.

LATE PERMIAN ERUPTIONS in Siberia lasted **2 million years,** covering an area the **SIZE OF AUSTRALIA** with **LAVA.**

70%
of **LAND-ANIMAL SPECIES** disappeared.

The **GREAT DYING,** also known as the Permian-Triassic Extinction, took place **251.9 million years ago.**

One **SURVIVOR** was
Lystrosaurus,
a **3FT-** (1m-) long, plant-eating, beaked **MAMMAL RELATIVE** with **2 TUSKLIKE TEETH.**

Lystrosaurus accounts for about **90%** of Early Triassic land vertebrate remains.

Coal comes from plant matter. A **10-MILLION-YEAR "COAL GAP"** in the geological record is evidence that many **forests perished,** perhaps due to **ACID RAIN AND WILDFIRES.**

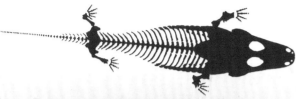

Early **AMPHIBIANS** called **TEMNOSPONDYLS** survived into the **TRIASSIC** and beyond. Some, such as **Mastodonsaurus,** resembled **CROCODILES** and grew up to **20FT** (6m) in length.

At least **8** **INSECT ORDERS DIED OUT,** including the **LARGEST-EVER DRAGONFLY** relatives, called **GRIFFENFLIES.**

THE GREAT DYING occurred over a period of about **60,000 years.**

As much as **90%** of **MARINE SPECIES WENT EXTINCT,** including **ALL** trilobites and eurypterids and **ALMOST ALL** ammonoids and gastropods.

Levels of the **GREENHOUSE GAS** **carbon dioxide** rose to **6 TIMES** its present-day level.

It took up to **10 million years** for **LIFE TO RECOVER** after the Great Dying, with the **ANCESTORS OF DINOSAURS AND MAMMALS, AMPHIBIANS,** and **ICHTHYOSAURS** taking hold.

TRIASSIC

Lystrosaurus was a distant **MAMMAL RELATIVE** that dominated the Early Triassic. Its discovery on **3 MODERN CONTINENTS** in the 1950s proved they were **ONCE CONNECTED.**

At the start of the Triassic, there was about **½** the level of **OXYGEN** found in today's air.

SUMMER TEMPERATURES
could have reached as high as

140°F
(60°C) during the **EARLY TRIASSIC PERIOD.**

THE BIGGEST TRIASSIC TREE FOSSIL in Arizona's Petrified Forest is **141FT** (43m) **LONG,** suggesting it may have grown up to **200FT** (60m)—as tall as a **20-STORY BUILDING.**

The **MOST RECENT** of several past **SUPERCONTINENTS,**

Pangea
existed for more than **100 MILLION YEARS.**

The **FIRST DINOSAURS** appeared around **20 MILLION** years into the Triassic Period.

Triassic fossils
from the bottom of the **TETHYS SEA** (that filled the C-shape of Pangea) were recently discovered

8,990FT
(2,740m) up in the **SWISS ALPS.**

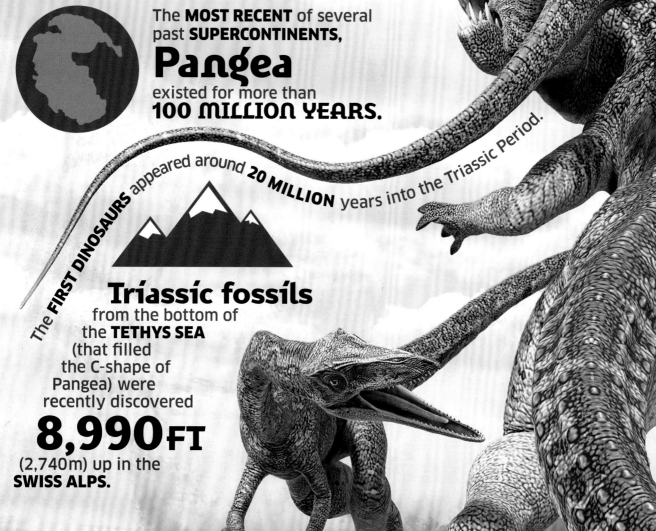

TRIASSIC WORLD

During the Triassic Period, almost all land was stuck together in one supercontinent called Pangea, surrounded by ocean. Much of Pangea was desertlike, but non-flowering plants, such as ferns, cycads, and conifers flourished to the north and south. Reptiles ruled the land, seas, and skies and included the first dinosaurs.

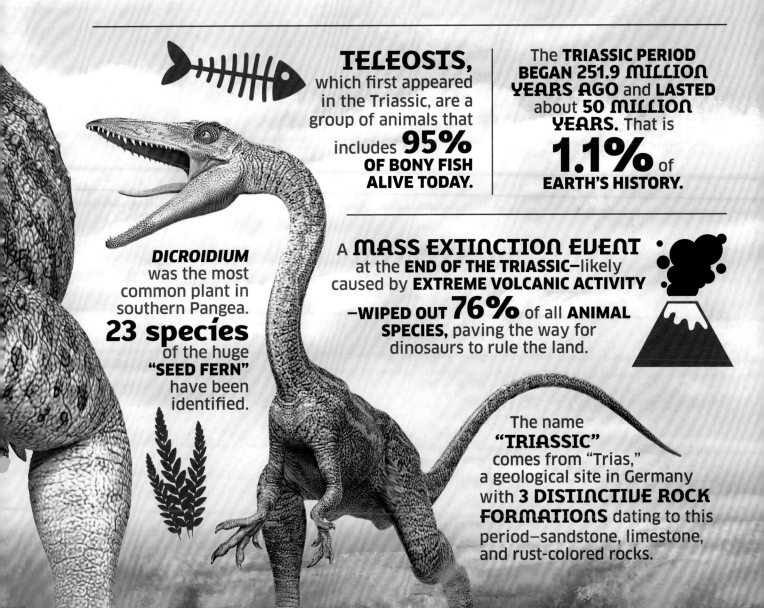

TELEOSTS, which first appeared in the Triassic, are a group of animals that includes **95% OF BONY FISH ALIVE TODAY.**

The **TRIASSIC PERIOD BEGAN 251.9 MILLION YEARS AGO** and **LASTED** about **50 MILLION YEARS.** That is **1.1%** of **EARTH'S HISTORY.**

DICROIDIUM was the most common plant in southern Pangea. **23 species** of the huge **"SEED FERN"** have been identified.

A **MASS EXTINCTION EVENT** at the **END OF THE TRIASSIC**—likely caused by **EXTREME VOLCANIC ACTIVITY** —**WIPED OUT 76%** of all **ANIMAL SPECIES,** paving the way for dinosaurs to rule the land.

The name **"TRIASSIC"** comes from "Trias," a geological site in Germany with **3 DISTINCTIVE ROCK FORMATIONS** dating to this period—sandstone, limestone, and rust-colored rocks.

Rauisuchian
REPTILES

Rauisuchians, such as the powerful *Postosuchus*, were early cousins of modern crocodiles, but their legs stood erect like pillars instead of sprawled out like today's crocs. Among the largest carnivorous reptiles of the Triassic, these bumpy-scaled predators ambushed early dinosaurs.

Estimates put **Fasolasuchus** as the **LARGEST MEAT-EATING REPTILE** of the Late Triassic. At

26—33 FT

(8–10m) long, it was nearly the **LENGTH OF A SCHOOL BUS.**

One **POSTOSUCHUS** fossil found in **1992** had the **REMAINS** of

4
different animals
in its **STOMACH.**

Each forelimb on **POSTOSUCHUS** had **5 DIGITS**, the

first
of which had a **LARGE CLAW.**

PRESTOSUCHUS was **FIRST DISCOVERED** in **BRAZIL** in **1928.** Another near-complete,

22 FT-

(6.7m-) long **FOSSIL SKELETON** of the creature was found there in **2010.**

The discovery of a group of **2 ADULT** and

10 young
POSTOSUCHUS SKELETONS suggests that the adults **PROTECTED** their **BABIES.**

MOST RAUISUCHIANS had rows of **PROTECTIVE OSTEODERMS** (bony skin plates) like modern crocs, but the enormous *Fasolasuchus* had only **1 SINGLE ROW** of tail scutes.

MOST RAUISUCHIAN reptiles **DIED OUT 200 MILLION YEARS AGO,** leaving **2-LEGGED THEROPOD** dinosaurs to become the **TOP LAND PREDATORS.**

Prestosuchus had **56 LONG, SERRATED TEETH,** which were replaced in **2 ALTERNATING WAVES,** first the odd teeth, then the even ones.

A study of **137 BITE-MARKED** *MASTODONSAURUS* **BONES** and **314** *BATRACHOTOMOS* **TEETH** showed that the latter **DISMEMBERED ITS PREY.**

One fossilized **POSTOSUCHUS ALISONAE TOOTH** measured **2¾IN** (7.2cm) long, the same as an **ADULT HUMAN THUMB.**

Postosuchus was discovered in Texas, in rocks dating to **220 MILLION YEARS AGO.**

BATRACHOTOMUS had short forelimbs only **70%** the size of its hindlimbs, which means they may have walked on **2 LEGS AS WELL AS 4.**

For an **APEX PREDATOR,** *SAUROSUCHUS* had a dainty bite, with a force of around **1,020 NEWTONS** —about **15 TIMES WEAKER** than that of today's **SALTWATER CROC.**

49

Nightmarish
NOTHOSAURS

The Triassic seas were home to a family of reptiles called nothosaurs. As they evolved from land animals into predators of the deep, their strong limbs became more flipperlike. Many, including *Nothosaurus*, had long flexible necks, so their heads could be twisted sideways to speedily snap up fish and squid.

Nothosaurus
could be up to
16 FT (5m)
in length and had a long, **MUSCULAR TAIL** for pushing itself **THROUGH THE WATER.**

Some **SCIENTISTS** think that
1
branch of **NOTHOSAURS EVOLVED** into **GIANT PLESIOSAURS**, such as *Liopleurodon.*

FOSSILIZED TRACKWAYS found in **CHINA** from
245
MILLION YEARS AGO
suggest that **NOTHOSAURS** used their **2 PADDLELIKE FRONT LEGS** to scoop out mud, uncovering **FISH AND SHRIMP TO EAT.**

NOTHOSAURUS
had **5**
SHORT CLAWS on each of its **4 WEBBED FEET** for **CLAMBERING** over **SLIPPERY ROCKS** on land.

One of the **SMALLEST-KNOWN NOTHOSAURS**, *Lariosaurus,* weighed just
22 LB (10kg).

There were around **12 species** of **Nothosaurus.** **FOSSILS** of the **REPTILE** have been discovered in **AFRICA, ASIA, AND EUROPE.**

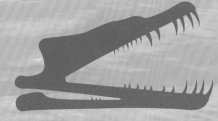

A **Nothosaurus zhangi FOSSIL** has been found with a **LOWER JAW** measuring **26IN** (65cm) in length—that's as **LONG AS A BULLDOG.**

Although **NOTHOSAURS THRIVED** during the **TRIASSIC PERIOD,** they all **DIED OUT** during a mass extinction around **200 million years ago.**

NOTHOSAURS had to come to the surface to breathe because they had **ZERO GILLS.**

With around **120** interlocking, **DAGGERLIKE TEETH, Nothosaurus** had no problems **GRIPPING** onto **SLIPPERY FISH** to eat.

Some nothosaurs, such as **LARIOSAURUS,** had **2 front flippers** much like those of a seal, **WITHOUT ANY DIGITS,** but still retained toes on their back feet.

Ceresiosaurus was **NOT** the **BIGGEST NOTHOSAUR** at **10FT** (3m) long, but it had **LONGER FLIPPERS** than any other.

Both **PETITE** and **2-LEGGED**, *EODROMAEUS* and *EORAPTOR* looked similar, but the **FIRST** is a forerunner to **THEROPODS** such as *T. rex*, while the **SECOND** is a forerunner to **SAUROPODS** such as *Diplodocus.*

Dinos found in Brazil's Santa Maria Formation range from **Pampadromaeus** at around **3 FT** (1m) to the **10 FT-**(3m-) long **Gnathovorax.**

Scans of fossils from **3 EARLY DINOSAURS**–*Buriolestes, Pampadromaeus,* and *Gnathovorax*–showed that their **BONES DID NOT YET HAVE AIR SACS** to make them lightweight like those of later dinos.

EARLY SAUROPODOMORPHS, the ancestors of huge **4-LEGGED SAUROPODS,** were the **MOST ABUNDANT** dinosaurs of the **LATE TRIASSIC.**

Early **SAUROPODOMORPHS** weighed in at under **110 LB** (50kg). By the end of the Triassic, **30 MILLION YEARS LATER,** some had grown to more than **5.5 TONS.**

The **FORELIMBS** (arms) of *EORAPTOR* are **1/2** the **LENGTH** of its **HINDLIMBS** (legs), showing it walked on **2 legs.**

The **EARLIEST-KNOWN UNDISPUTED DINOSAURS** have been found in **2 PLACES: Brazil** and **Argentina.**

A fragmented skeleton of **EODROMAEUS** excavated in **1996** took **15 years** to reconstruct.

Dating to **231.4 million years ago,** *PANPHAGIA* got its name, meaning **"EAT ALL,"** because this early **SAUROPOD** relative still had an **OMNIVOROUS DIET.**

Early DINOSAURS

The oldest-known dinosaurs evolved from small but speedy reptiles called dinosauromorphs in southern Pangea around 240 million years ago. They lacked distinctive features, such as plates or spikes, seen in later species. These early dinosaurs could run on two legs, steering clear of larger crocodilelike predators of the Late Triassic.

Of the **7 EARLY DINOSAUR SPECIES** found in **BRAZIL'S SANTA MARIA FORMATION,**

5

were discovered in the **21ST CENTURY.**

The **earliest-confirmed dinosaur remains** are from around **233 MILLION YEARS AGO,** but there were already **MULTIPLE SPECIES** then, so they must have **EVOLVED EVEN EARLIER.**

Dating to **243 million years ago,** AFRICA'S *Nyasasaurus* is a candidate for **CLOSEST DINO RELATIVE.**

EARLY DINOSAURS were similarly sized and **COMPARATIVELY SMALL,** mostly **20-75LB (10-35kg).** Eventually, the biggest dino would be up to

35 million times

HEAVIER than the **SMALLEST.**

At **4FT** (1.2m) long from nose to tail, *EODROMAEUS* would have only stood about **KNEE-HEIGHT** to an **ADULT HUMAN.**

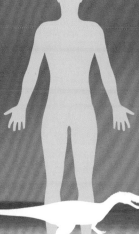

The **SKULL** of the first fossil *Eoraptor* measured just **4⁴/₅IN** (12.3cm) in length, slightly longer than a **FOX SKULL**.

EORAPTOR was an omnivore with more than **70 teeth**— **LEAF-SHAPED ONES** for snipping plants and **BACKWARD-CURVING, SERRATED TEETH** for slicing meat.

The **EYE SOCKET** **1/4** spans of the skull, suggesting *Eoraptor* had **LARGE EYES** on the side of its head for **GOOD ALL-ROUND VISION**.

The **first skeleton** was discovered by curator **RICARDO MARTÍNEZ** when he spotted **2 teeth** sticking out of a **FIST-SIZED BALL OF ROCK** surrounded by a layer of **IRON ORE**.

Eoraptor is one of **7 types** of dinosaurs discovered in **ISCHIGUALASTO,** showing there was already significant **DINOSAUR DIVERSITY** when it lived.

It took **4 years** to prepare the **FIRST SPECIMEN** for display.

A nearby **VOLCANIC ASH BED** helped scientists date *EORAPTOR* to around **231 million years ago,** the **BEGINNING** of the **AGE OF DINOSAURS.**

EORAPTOR got its name, meaning **"DAWN THIEF,"** for its early origin and its **5-FINGERED HANDS** with **3 long claws.**

Found in **1991,** *Eoraptor* is still one of the **MOST COMPLETE VERTEBRATE SKELETONS** ever discovered in the **ISCHIGUALASTO FORMATION.**

THE FIRST SPECIMEN was shipped more than **5,200 MILES** (8,370km) north from **SAN JUAN, ARGENTINA,** to the **FIELD MUSEUM** in **CHICAGO, ILLINOIS,** for preparation.

EORAPTOR

Unearthed from Argentina's famous Ischigualasto Formation, *Eoraptor lunesis* is one of the most primitive dinosaurs discovered. It lived in the lush floodplains of southwestern Pangea, and although it looks like a small two-legged theropod, it is now believed to be a forerunner of huge four-legged sauropods such as *Brachiosaurus*.

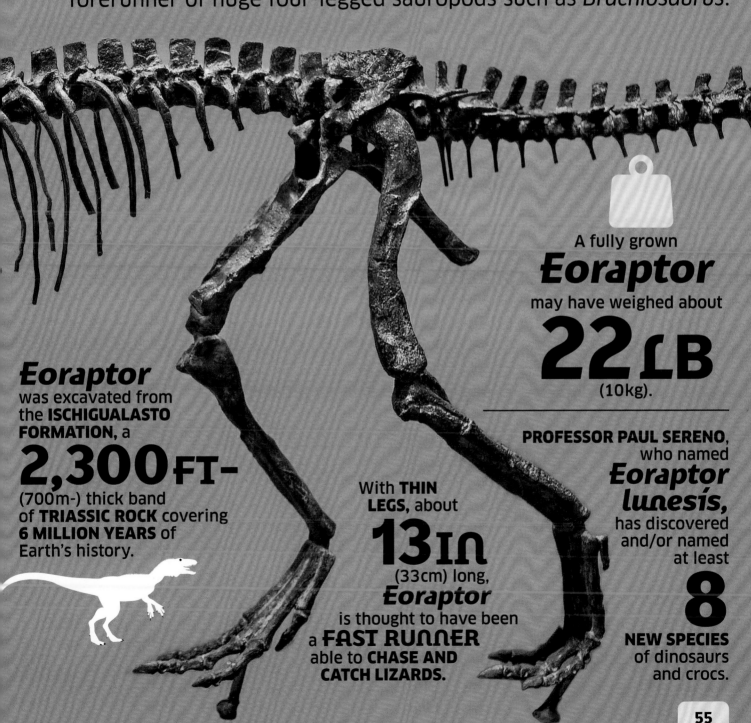

A fully grown
Eoraptor
may have weighed about
22 LB
(10kg).

Eoraptor
was excavated from
the **ISCHIGUALASTO
FORMATION**, a
2,300 FT-
(700m-) thick band
of **TRIASSIC ROCK** covering
6 MILLION YEARS of
Earth's history.

With **THIN
LEGS**, about
13 IN
(33cm) long,
Eoraptor
is thought to have been
a **FAST RUNNER**
able to **CHASE AND
CATCH LIZARDS.**

PROFESSOR PAUL SERENO,
who named
*Eoraptor
lunesis,*
has discovered
and/or named
at least
8
NEW SPECIES
of dinosaurs
and crocs.

Hungry
HERRERASAURIDS

The Triassic Period saw the dawn of the Age of the Dinosaurs—and herrerasaurids were some of the first to evolve. These two-legged carnivores had sharp teeth that curved backward for dragging prey. They prowled southern Pangea for around six million years.

HERRERASAURUS FOSSILS were first found in

1958,

and the dinosaur was **NAMED AFTER** the **GOAT FARMER** who discovered them, **Victorino Herrera.**

The **LARGEST** of the **EARLIEST-KNOWN DINOSAURS**, the **PONY-SIZED**

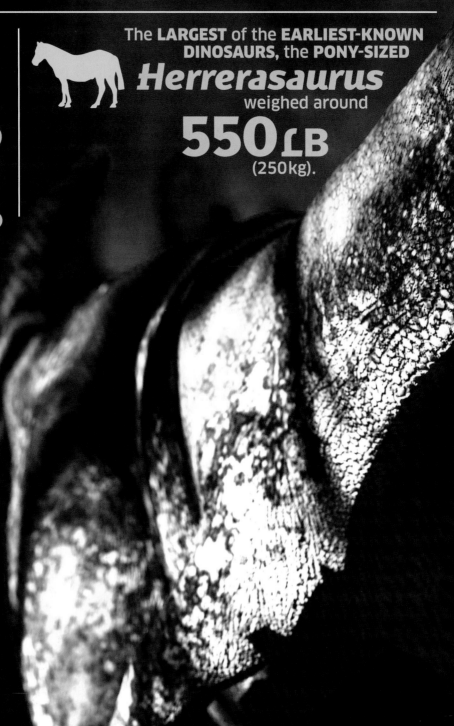

Herrerasaurus

weighed around

550LB

(250kg).

HERRERASAURUS had

5 toes

on each foot, but the **OUTER 2** did not carry its weight, hinting at the **EVOLUTION** to the

3-toed feet

MANY DINOSAURS had.

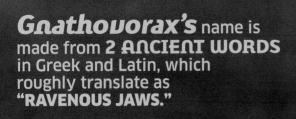

Gnathovorax's name is made from **2 ANCIENT WORDS** in Greek and Latin, which roughly translate as "RAVENOUS JAWS."

Only **1 species** of *HERRERASAURUS* —*H. ISCHIGUALASTENSIS*—has been found, but some paleontologists think lots of other **DINOSAURS EVOLVED FROM IT.**

HERRERASAURUS had sturdy legs that were **2 times** as long as its arms.

An agile hunter, *HERRERASAURUS*

Herrerasaurus had a **SECOND HINGE** or flexible joint on each side of its **BOTTOM JAW,** which helped it clamp down on struggling prey.

Slender *STAURIKOSAURUS* weighed around **66 LB** (30kg). It **ATE LIZARDS** and **SCAVENGED THE PREY** of other, larger predators.

The **10FT-** (3m-) long carnivore *SANJUANSAURUS* was **NOT AN APEX PREDATOR**— it was no match for the huge reptile *SAUROSUCHUS,* which was **MORE THAN** **2 times** **ITS LENGTH.**

There is a debate about where *Herrerasaurus* fits on the **DINOSAUR FAMILY TREE** or if it was a dinosaur at all. Most experts now believe it to be an **EARLY SAURISCHIAN,** the dino group that includes both **2-LEGGED THEROPODS** and **4-LEGGED SAUROPODS.**

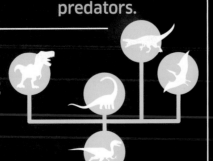

The **FIRST NEAR-COMPLETE** *Herrerasaurus* **SKELETON** was spotted in 1988, in sandstone dating to **230 million years ago.**

Over **100** fossilized skeletons of **Plateosaurus** have been found, mostly in **GERMANY**.

The **LARGEST** *Plateosaurus* ever discovered measured

33FT

(10m) in length, as long as a **STRETCH LIMO.**

In **1978**, a clutch of

6

2½IN- (6.5cm-) **LONG** *Massospondylus* **EGGS** were discovered in **SOUTH AFRICA.**

Plateosaurus had **EFFICIENT LUNGS** that could **INHALE** about

5 gallons

(20 liters) of **AIR** in **1 BREATH.**

The **OLDEST DINOSAUR EMBRYOS** ever found are

190-million-year-old *Massospondylus* BABIES measuring

6IN

(15cm) **LONG.**

Thecodontosaurus was only the **fifth dinosaur** to be named, in **1836,**

6 years

before the term **"DINOSAUR"** was used.

The **REMAINS** of the

6FT 6IN-

(2m-) **LONG** prosauropod

Thecodontosaurus

have often been found in **"FISSURE FILLS"**—gaps in the earth where bones were washed into and then buried.

Epic
PROSAUROPODS

These long-necked, small-skulled dinosaurs were early relatives of huge four-legged sauropods. Prosauropods, such as *Plateosaurus*, were generally smaller with shorter forelimbs than their sauropod descendants and could walk on either two or four legs.

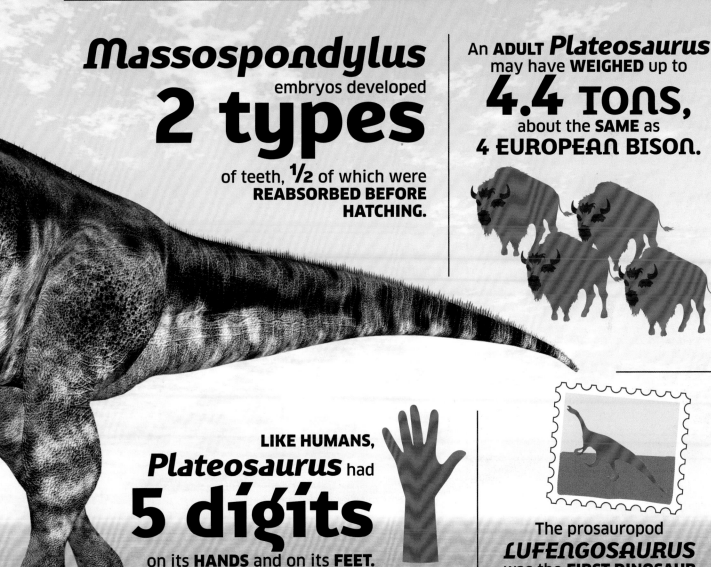

Massospondylus embryos developed **2 types** of teeth, **½** of which were **REABSORBED BEFORE HATCHING.**

An **ADULT** *Plateosaurus* may have **WEIGHED** up to **4.4 TONS,** about the **SAME** as **4 EUROPEAN BISON.**

LIKE HUMANS, *Plateosaurus* had **5 digits** on its **HANDS** and on its **FEET.**

Plateosaurus had more than **100 LEAF-SHAPED TEETH** it used to **SNIP PLANTS,** such as **FERNS** and **CYCADS.**

The prosauropod *LUFENGOSAURUS* was the **FIRST DINOSAUR** to star on a **POSTAGE STAMP.** After a complete skeleton was discovered in **1958,** it appeared on a Chinese **8-yuan stamp.**

Peculiar PLACODONTS

This group of mollusk-eating marine reptiles first appeared around 246 million years ago. As the predators around them got bigger, placodonts developed bony plates to keep safe. However, the plates couldn't protect them from the Late Triassic extinctions—no placodont survived those.

6 FT-

(1.8m-) long **PSEPHODERMA** had a short, narrow **POKERLIKE SNOUT** to **PROBE FOR PREY** on the seafloor.

One of the **heaviest placodonts** at

500 LB

(227kg), **PLACODUS** had **DENSE BONES** that would have helped it **SINK TO THE SEAFLOOR** and feed with little effort.

Besides its **2 TRUE EYES**, *Placodus* had a **third** **EYELIKE STRUCTURE ON TOP OF ITS HEAD**, which was probably used to **SENSE LIGHT** and **HELP WITH ORIENTATION**.

PLACODUS means **"FLAT TOOTH"** because of the

6

LARGE, FLATTENED TEETH forming a **CRUSHING ZONE** on its upper palate.

Much of **CYAMODUS'S ARMOR** was made from **6-sided osteoderms** (bony skin plates).

Only 1

PLACODONT is known to have lived outside an ocean environment. **Henodus** lived in **LAGOONS** and **PONDS**.

HENODUS only had

2 teeth

in each jaw, but also **BRISTLELIKE BALEEN**, suggesting it might have been a **FILTER FEEDER**, trapping food particles to eat.

At **3-10 FT** (1-3m), **placodonts** weren't giants, but they did **LOOK LIKE** very **LARGE TURTLES.**

When the **FIRST PLACODONT** was discovered in **1830,** it was **THOUGHT TO BE** a **FISH.**

With its **WEBBED, 5-toed HANDS** and **FEET** and **STRONG TAIL,** *Placodus* was a **GOOD SWIMMER** but quite **CLUMSY ON LAND.**

Psephoderma's **ARMORED SHELL** was divided into **2 PARTS.**

PLACODONT ARMOR hardened in later life, but not quickly enough for

the **2** **YOUNG** *CYAMODUS* that were found **IN THE STOMACH** of a fossilized *Lariosaurus.*

Henodus was **3 FT 3 IN** (1 m) **LONG** and **3 FT 3 IN** (1 m) **WIDE** and shaped like a **MODERN TURTLE.**

PLACODONT FOSSILS have been **FOUND** on

3 **CONTINENTS: EUROPE, AFRICA,** and **ASIA.**

TOP 5
BIGGEST
SWIMMERS

Marine reptiles evolved to be very big very quickly. Perhaps due to plentiful prey, Triassic seas gave rise to Earth's first true giants, while the longest ever mosasaurs and plesiosaurs arrived in the Cretaceous.

SHONISAURUS SIKANNIENSIS
Late Triassic • **BRITISH COLUMBIA, CANADA**
Length: **69FT** (21m)

1

Discovered in 1997 along the banks of the Sikanni Chief River, this 210-million-year-old ichthyosaur was a monster sea predator. It likely feasted on other marine reptiles and weighed at least 90 tons.

2 ### CYMBOSPONDYLUS YOUNGORUM
Middle Triassic • **NEVADA, US**
Length: **56FT** (17m)

When a 6ft 6in- (2m-) long ichythosaur skull was unearthed in the Augusta Mountains of Nevada in 2014, the creature it came from was dubbed "Earth's first ocean giant." Dating to 246 million years ago, it is the largest fossil from its era.

3 ### MOSASAURUS HOFFMANNII
Late Cretaceous • **NETHERLANDS AND MOROCCO**
Length: **56FT** (17m)

This carnivorous monster was likely still swimming in the Tethys Sea when the dinosaurs went extinct 66 million years ago. The first mosasaur found, it was uncovered in a Dutch chalk quarry in 1762 and mistaken for a whale and a crocodile before being named as its own species in 1829.

4 ### HIMALAYASAURUS TIBETENSIS
Late Triassic • **TIBET, CHINA**
Length: **50FT** (15m)

Named after the mountainous region where it was discovered in 1972, *Himalayasaurus* is known only from skull fragments, fin bones, and a few vertebrae. Related to giant shastasaurids such as *Shonisaurus*, it was estimated to exceed 50ft (15m) in length.

5 ### ALBERTONECTES VANDERVELDEI
Late Cretaceous • **ALBERTA, CANADA**
Length: **38FT** (11.5m)

Albertonectes is a genus of extremely long-necked plesiosaurs known as elasmosaurids. This species has the distinction of holding the title for the longest neck of any marine reptile at 23ft (7m), taking up most of its overall length. A near-complete fossil boasts all 132 of its vertebrae.

Coelophysis

had **2 UNUSUALLY LARGE, FORWARD-FACING EYES,** which would have helped it watch for **PREDATORS AND PREY** from long distances.

COELOPHYSIS had more than

50

SAWLIKE TEETH THAT POINTED BACKWARD, making it difficult for prey to escape its jaws.

A **210-million-year-old COELOPHYSIS SKULL** was sent into space on board the shuttle **ENDEAVOUR** on **JANUARY 22, 1998.**

There are **2 forms** of **COELOPHYSIS.** One has a longer skull and neck, which might suggest **MALES WERE BIGGER THAN FEMALES...** or the other way round.

Fossil bones from up to

1,000

COELOPHYSIS BAURI were unearthed in a quarry at **GHOST RANCH**, New Mexico. This is the **BIGGEST MASS GRAVE OF ANY DINOSAUR SPECIES.**

Coelophysis

had a **FOURTH DIGIT** on each hand that it **DIDN'T USE FOR ANYTHING.**

COELOPHYSIS had **2 LONG HIND LEGS** and would probably have reached speeds of up to

25 MPH

(40kph).

Speedy
COELOPHYSIS

This Late Triassic dinosaur's name is taken from Greek words meaning "hollow form"—because it had hollow bones. *Coelophysis's* small, lightweight frame made it a fast hunter. The birdlike carnivore had a long, S-shaped neck, which it could snap straight to seize prey.

New Mexico, the **47TH** state of the US, adopted *Coelophysis* as its state fossil in **1981**.

It was thought *Coelophysis* was a **CANNIBAL**, but **FURTHER STUDY** of **2 skeletons** proved the **OPPOSITE** —any **BONES INSIDE THE DINOSAURS' STOMACH** came from **OTHER SPECIES.**

In **2021**, scientists used a **COELOPHYSIS BAURI** simulation to show that **2-LEGGED DINOSAURS** probably **WAGGED THEIR TAILS** as they ran to help **KEEP THEIR BALANCE.**

Coelophysis had **3 LONG, CLAWED FINGERS** on each hand, which were perfect for **GRABBING** onto **PREY**, such as **REPTILES AND FISH.**

COELOPHYSIS walked on **3 toes** in a **SIMILAR WAY** to modern game birds, such as **GUINEA FOWL.**

COELOPHYSIS could reach **10FT** (3m) long and **WEIGHED** up to **110LB** (50kg).

The **8IN-** (20cm-) long *BRASILODON QUADRANGULARIS* is one of the **CLOSEST-KNOWN RELATIVES** of early mammals. It lived in what is now **BRAZIL** **225 million years ago.**

Megazostrodon

had a **SKULL** similar to that of an **OPOSSUM**, but the whole animal was a **TINY** **4IN** (10cm) in length.

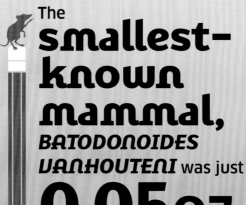

The **smallest-known mammal,** *BATODONOIDES VANHOUTENI* was just **0.05oz** (1.3g) in **WEIGHT**. It was the size of a **PENCIL ERASER.**

A total of **22** *Filikomys* **SKELETONS** were found on Egg Mountain, a dinosaur nesting site in Montana, clustered in **MIXED-AGE GROUPS** of **2–5**, showing that, **UNLIKE 70% OF TODAY'S MAMMALS,** they were social creatures.

Early mammals had **4 TYPES OF TEETH—** **INCISORS, CANINES, PREMOLARS,** and **MOLARS–** that allowed them to **grab, slice, and chew food.**

Zalambdalestes,

from **LATE CRETACEOUS MONGOLIA,** was **8IN** (20cm) long and may have hopped like a **JERBOA** on its **LONG HIND LEGS.**

One of the **LARGER EARLY MAMMALS,** rat-sized *Sinoconodon* weighed up to **18oz** (517g).

The first
MAMMALS

During the Triassic Period, the first mammals began scurrying around Earth. Many looked like shrews and fed on insects and small reptiles, coming out at night to avoid getting snapped up by dinosaurs. These early mammals likely laid eggs but were warm-blooded and raised their young on milk.

Morganucodon was a **LATE TRIASSIC BURROWING CREATURE** about **3½IN** (9cm) long with a tail **½** **ITS BODY LENGTH.**

The shrewlike **MORGANUCODON WEIGHED A MAXIMUM** of **3OZ** (80g).

Sinoconodon was a **193-MILLION-YEAR-OLD MAMMAL ANCESTOR** with a **2⅖IN-** (6.2cm-) long **SKULL.**

MORGANUCODON is estimated to have lived to around **14 YEARS.**

The **EARLIEST-KNOWN REMAINS** of **placental mammals,** which gave birth to **LIVE YOUNG** instead of laying eggs, date to **145 MILLION YEARS AGO.**

JURASSIC

JURASSIC WORLD

Around 200 million years ago a supercontinent split in two, sea levels and temperatures were high, and reptiles continued their domination of the land, sea, and air. The Jurassic Period saw the rise of large predators, such as allosaurs, as well as the first stegosaurs, birds, and gigantic sauropods.

The name **"JURASSIC"** comes from **SWITZERLAND'S JURA MOUNTAINS,** where rocks of this period were **FIRST IDENTIFIED IN**

1795.

THE JURASSIC PERIOD was **WARM AND HUMID,** with summer **TEMPERATURES** averaging

86°F

(30°C).

The **OLDEST-SURVIVING SPECIES OF TREE** is the maidenhair, *Ginkgo biloba,* a Jurassic tree from about **160 MILLION YEARS AGO.**

The **Jurassic Period** lasted from **201.3–145 MILLION YEARS AGO.**

The **"FIRST BIRD"** or birdlike dinosaur, **ARCHAEOPTERYX,** emerged about

150 MILLION YEARS AGO

in **GERMANY,** when it was part of an island group in a **TROPICAL SEA.**

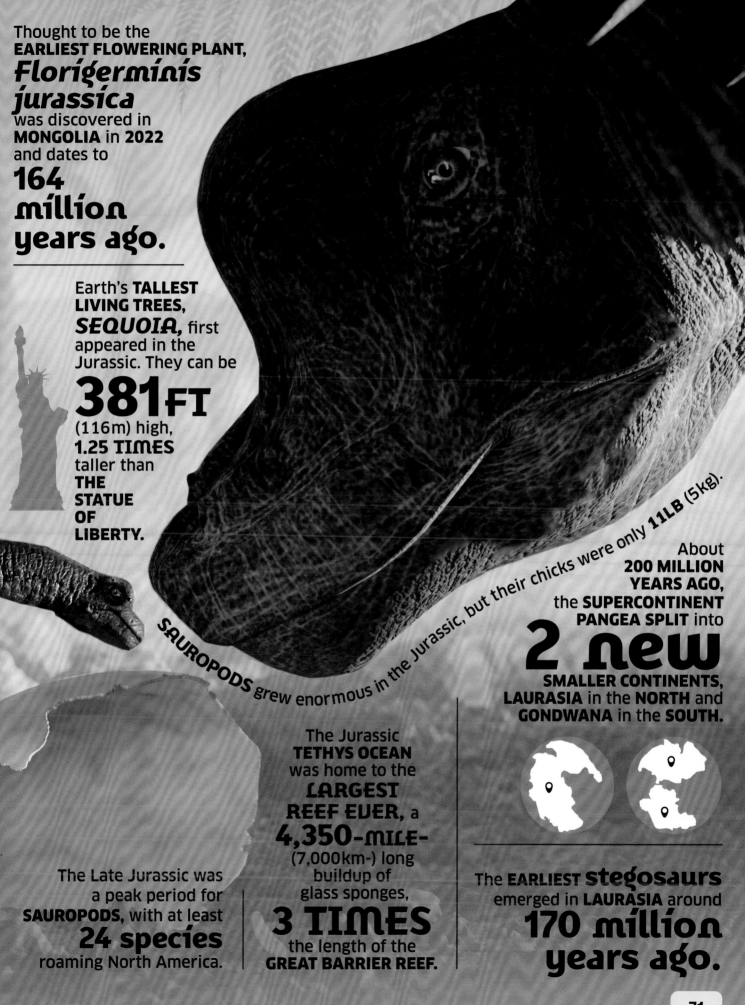

Thought to be the **EARLIEST FLOWERING PLANT,** *Florigerminis jurassica* was discovered in **MONGOLIA** in **2022** and dates to **164 million years ago.**

Earth's **TALLEST LIVING TREES, SEQUOIA,** first appeared in the Jurassic. They can be **381FT** (116m) high, **1.25 TIMES** taller than **THE STATUE OF LIBERTY.**

SAUROPODS grew enormous in the Jurassic, but their chicks were only **11LB** (5kg).

About **200 MILLION YEARS AGO,** the **SUPERCONTINENT PANGEA SPLIT** into **2 new SMALLER CONTINENTS, LAURASIA** in the **NORTH** and **GONDWANA** in the **SOUTH.**

The Late Jurassic was a peak period for **SAUROPODS,** with at least **24 species** roaming North America.

The Jurassic **TETHYS OCEAN** was home to the **LARGEST REEF EVER,** a **4,350-MILE-** (7,000km-) long buildup of glass sponges, **3 TIMES** the length of the **GREAT BARRIER REEF.**

The **EARLIEST stegosaurs** emerged in **LAURASIA** around **170 million years ago.**

Early Jurassic
NEOTHEROPODS

The only group of theropods to survive the Triassic-Jurassic extinction event 201.4 million years ago were the neotheropods. This diverse bunch of two-legged dinosaurs with blade-sharp teeth included the largest land-based carnivores of the Early Jurassic, such as *Dilophosaurus* and *Cryolophosaurus.*

A **DOUBLE-CRESTED NEOTHEROPOD** discovered in **CHINA** in **1938** was named *Sinosaurus triassicus,* but was later found to date to **199 MILLION YEARS AGO** in the Early Jurassic, **NOT THE TRIASSIC.**

At more than **21**FT (6.5m) long, the **FAN-CRESTED *CRYOLOPHOSAURUS*** is the **LARGEST-KNOWN THEROPOD** from the **EARLY JURASSIC.**

DILOPHOSAURUS'S name means "**2-CRESTED LIZARD.**"

A study of **60** *DILOPHOSAURUS* foot fragments found **NO FRACTURES**, suggesting that this carnivore was light on its feet.

Dílophosaurus weighed up to **1,000 LB** (450kg), but, like other **NEOTHEROPODS**, its **BONES HAD AIR POCKETS** that kept its skeleton **LIGHT.**

Around **2,000 FOSSILIZED FOOTPRINTS** have been found at **DINOSAUR STATE PARK** in Connecticut that likely belong to **Dílophosaurus.**

The **FIRST JURASSIC PARK** film, released in **1993**, features a **Dílophosaurus** that has an **EXTENDABLE NECK FRILL** and can **SPIT VENOM,** but there is **zero** proof for either.

The petite **Tachíraptor** was only **5FT** (1.5m) long and is one of the few dinosaurs to have been found in **VENEZUELA.**

SHUANGBAISAURUS lived in what is now China, but **ONLY 1** **21IN-** (54cm-) long **PARTIAL SKULL** has been found so far.

Excavated at **13,330 FT** (4,100m) above sea level from a site **400 MILES** (640km) from the **SOUTH POLE,** **CRYOLOPHOSAURUS** was the **FIRST CARNIVOROUS DINOSAUR** found in **ANTARCTICA.**

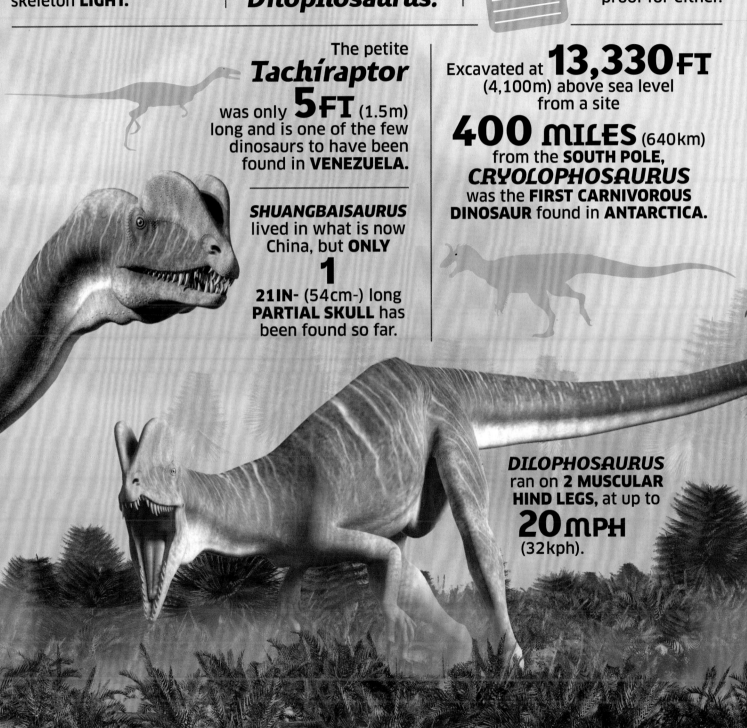

DILOPHOSAURUS ran on **2 MUSCULAR HIND LEGS,** at up to **20 MPH** (32kph).

Scary
CERATOSAURS

This diverse group of theropod dinosaurs lived from the Early Jurassic to the Late Cretaceous. Ceratosaurs were fast on two long legs and ranged in size from the barely waist-high, omnivorous *Limusaurus* to the massive bull-horned meat-eater *Carnotaurus*.

CERATOSAURUS had **KNIFELIKE TEETH** that grew to more than **3½IN** (9cm) **LONG.**

CERATOSAURUS'S name means **"HORNED LIZARD"** after the **SPIKE ON ITS NOSE.** The horn **GREW UP TO**

3IN
(7cm) long.

Identified only by the **TIP OF ITS DEADLY SNOUT,** packed with long, curved teeth, *GENYODECTES* became the **first theropod** discovered in **SOUTH AMERICA**, in 1901.

Ceratosaurus was **UNUSUAL** for a theropod because it had a row of small **OSTEODERMS** (skin bones) running down its back. They were up to **1½IN-** (3.8cm-) tall on its tail.

A fully grown **Ceratosaurus** may have **WEIGHED** about **2,160LB** (980kg), close to the **HEAVIEST POLAR BEAR ON RECORD.**

RUNNING on **2 LEGS,** *CARNOTAURUS* may have **REACHED SPEEDS** of up to **25MPH** (40kph) over short distances.

A team **IN CHINA** found **19 specimens** of *LIMUSAURUS* from **6 DIFFERENT AGE GROUPS,** which showed its **TEETH** were **REPLACED BY A BEAK** as it aged.

Carnotaurus had **VERY SHORT ARMS.** They were about **20IN** (50cm) long, just

12%

the length of its legs.

Compared to its body, **Ceratosaurus HAD A LARGE HEAD.** The skull measured **24IN** (60cm) long, the length of **2 SUB SANDWICHES.**

First uncovered in **TANZANIA** in

1920,

ELAPHROSAURUS was only recognized as a ceratosaur in

2016,

when a **MUSEUM RENOVATION** gave paleontologists the chance to **EXAMINE THE SKELETON.**

One of the **TOP PREDATORS OF THE LATE JURASSIC,** at

23FT (7m) long,

CERATOSAURUS was only about ⅔ the size of the later **T. REX.**

Majungasaurus
may have **REPLACED** its **WHOLE SET OF TEETH** every

2 MONTHS.

The tail of a **CERATOSAURUS** contained more than

50 VERTEBRAE

and made up about

½

of its total **BODY LENGTH.**

MAJUNGASAURUS was one of the **LAST-KNOWN THEROPODS.** It lived during the **FINAL 4 million years** before the **EXTINCTION EVENT** that wiped out nonavian dinosaurs 66 million years ago.

Mamenchisaurus hochuanensis

WEIGHED about **16.5 TONS**, the equivalent of **6 hippos.**

A **MAMENCHISAURUS** neck contained **19 VERTEBRAE**, the **MOST OF ANY DINOSAUR.** By comparison, a **GIRAFFE** has just **7 neck bones.**

To maintain its weight, **MAMENCHISAURUS** would have had to eat about **1,150 LB** (520kg) of vegetation a day, equivalent to around **6,500 HUMAN SERVINGS OF SPINACH.**

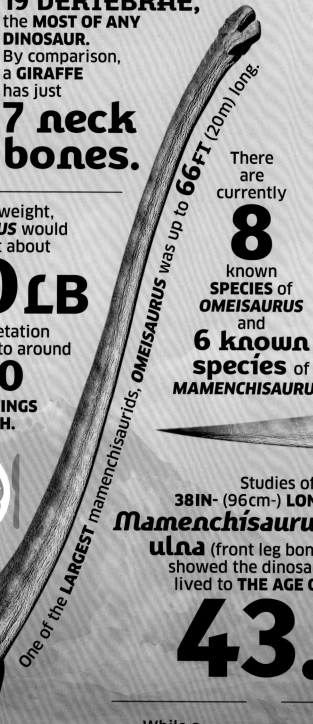

One of the **LARGEST** mamenchisaurids, **OMEISAURUS** was up to **66FT** (20m) long.

There are currently **8** known **SPECIES** of **OMEISAURUS** and **6 known species** of **MAMENCHISAURUS.**

Known only from a tail excavated in **1912** in **TANZANIA**, the **150–MILLION –YEAR–OLD** *Wamweracaudia* was the **FIRST MAMENCHISAURID** found outside Asia.

Studies of a **38IN-** (96cm-) **LONG** **Mamenchisaurus ulna** (front leg bone) showed the dinosaur lived to **THE AGE OF** **43.**

Plant-eating **MAMENCHISAURIDS** may have released more than **700 gallons** (2,650 liters) of **METHANE GAS** each day through **BURPS AND FARTS.**

While a **MAMENCHISAURUS** neck was **LONG**, its neck **BONES** were **LIGHT**, up to **77%** **FILLED WITH AIR, LIKE** those of **birds.**

Marvelous
MAMENCHISAURIDS

These distinctive sauropods had ultra-long necks, accounting for up to half of their total body length. Dating from the Jurassic and Early Cretaceous Periods, mamenchisaurids have been discovered in Asia and Africa and include some of the largest animals ever.

The **LARGEST MAMENCHISAURID** may be **CHINA'S** *MAMENCHISAURUS SINOCANADORUM.* It is estimated to have been

85FT
(26m) **LONG.**

A *Mamenchisaurus youngi* **SKULL** that included most of its **PADDLE-SHAPED TEETH** showed it had

44 TEETH
in its **UPPER JAW** and
48 in its **LOWER JAW.**

MAMENCHISAURUS HOCHUANENSIS had a **TAIL CLUB.** However, with an **IMPACT FORCE** of only

450 NEWTONS,
the club was **PROBABLY NOT USED FOR DEFENSE.**

A **1974** dig at a quarry in **ZIGONG, CHINA,** revealed bones from at least **13** *OMEISAURUS* that were assembled into **2 SKELETONS.**

OMEISAURUS TIANFUENSIS had one of the **LONGEST NECKS** compared to body size of any animal. At **30 FT** (9.1m) long, it made up **½** of its **OVERALL BODY LENGTH.**

TOP 5 LONGEST NECKS

The tallest animals of all time were gargantuan, four-legged sauropod dinosaurs that fed on treetops. Most often, paleontologists estimate their height from a few surviving bones.

1

MAMENCHISAURUS SINOCANADORUM
Late Jurassic • Xinjiang, China
Estimated neck length: **50FT** (15m)

Around 162 million years ago, a sauropod with a neck six times longer than that of the tallest giraffe thundered through the forests of Asia. Scientists calculated its neck size in 2023 based on a few vertebrae found in 1987.

2

SUPERSAURUS VIVIANAE • Late Jurassic • US
Estimated neck length: **50FT** (15m)

One estimate puts this enormous North American sauropod as the longest dinosaur yet found, with a neck the same size as that of *Mamenchisaurus* and a tail that was even longer! The species name comes from Vivian Jones, the amateur paleontologist who discovered it in 1972.

3

XINJIANGTITAN SHANSHANESIS • Middle Jurassic
Xinjiang, China • Neck length: **14.9FT** (49m)

Named after the Chinese region where it was discovered, this titanic Xinjiang fossil boasts the longest complete neck of any dinosaur to date. With 18 massive vertebrae, it was used as a comparison to help calculate the neck size of the closely related *Mamenchisaurus*.

4

SAUROPOSEIDON PROTELES • Early Cretaceous • US
Estimated neck length: **40FT** (12m)

First identified by some enormous neck bones found in the state of Oklahoma in 1994, *Sauroposeidon* may have reached 60ft (18m) in height. Its name refers to Poseidon, the Greek god of earthquakes (as well as the sea), because it must have caused tremors with each step.

5

DREADNOUGHTUS SCHRANI • Late Cretaceous
Patagonia, Argentina • Estimated neck length: **36FT** (11m)

This South American titanosaur whose name means "fear nothing" dates to 77 million years ago. *Dreadnoughtus*, most recently estimated to have weighed 53 tons, temporarily took the title for heaviest land animal when it was first described in 2014.

Staggering
STEGOSAURS

These large, four-legged herbivores with narrow heads and hooflike toes lived in woodlands during the Middle Jurassic to Early Cretaceous. They are known for their two rows of bony backplates, but it is still a mystery what exactly they were used for!

Stegosaurus armatus is the **BIGGEST STEGOSAUR.** It reached

30FT
(9m)–about the length of **2 cars.**

Miragaia has the **LONGEST NECK** of any **STEGOSAUR,** with at least

17
VERTEBRAE that made up **⅓** of its **BODY LENGTH.**

The **FIRST STEGOSAUR EVER DISCOVERED,** ***Dacentrurus*** was **FOUND IN A CLAY PIT** in **ENGLAND** in **1874.**

A study of **51 *STEGOSAURUS* TAIL SPIKES** showed that **10%** of them were **HEALING** from **BROKEN TIPS,** suggesting they were successfully used for **DEFENSE AGAINST PREDATORS.**

The **4-SPIKED TAIL** of many **STEGOSAURS** is sometimes called a **thagomizer,** a term that scientists adopted from a **COMIC STRIP!**

STEGOSAUR BONES

have been found on **5 CONTINENTS—** all except **AUSTRALIA AND ANTARCTICA.**

STEGOSAURUS had **17–22 PLATES** called **SCUTES** made from a **LACY BONY MATERIAL** sheathed in **HORN.**

STEGOSAURUS PLATES

varied widely in size, and each one was **UNIQUE.** The **LARGEST** were found over the hips and could be more than

3FT (1m) tall.

The **EARLIEST-KNOWN STEGOSAUR,** *Bashanosaurus primitivus,* was unearthed in **CHINA** in **2022** and dates to

168 million

years ago.

TENDAGURU IN TANZANIA

has yielded **900** *Kentrosaurus* bones from **MANY DIFFERENT ANIMALS,** which have been put together to form **2 SKELETONS** for display at museums.

Stegosaurs

had very **SMALL BRAINS** for their size. *Stegosaurus's* was shaped a bit like a **"BENT HOTDOG"** and was around **80 G** (3oz), about **0.001%** of its body weight.

Clomping
CAMARASAURIDS

Camarasaurids were sauropods that lived mostly in North America. Compared to giants such as *Diplodocus* and *Titanosaurus*, these four-legged Jurassic plant-eaters were relatively small with shorter necks and legs, as well as bigger heads and bellies.

Camarasaurus
REPLACED ITS TEETH every

62

DAYS or so.

A *CAMARASAURUS* **TAIL** included

53
VERTEBRAE.

A **SKELETAL RECONSTRUCTION** of
Camarasaurus
was **PAINTED LIFE-SIZE** on a canvas measuring

52 FT
(16m) long.

CAMARASAURUS reached adulthood at **20 years** and lived up to **35.**

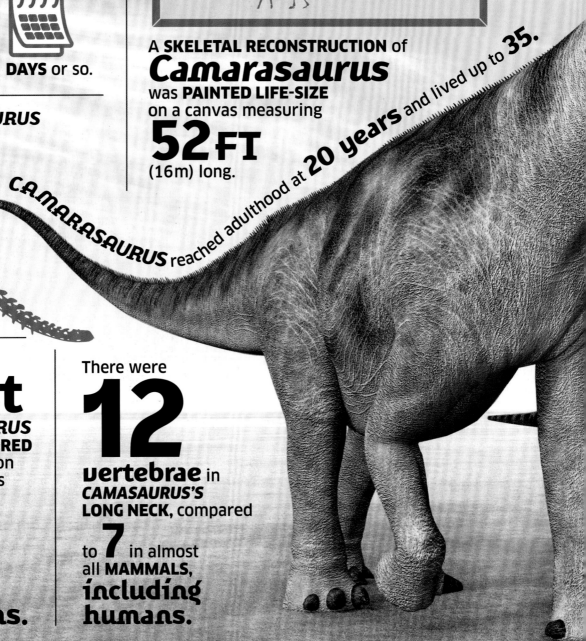

The **first** *CAMARASAURUS* **FOSSILS DISCOVERED** were a collection of loose bones from about

6
specimens.

There were

12
vertebrae in *CAMASAURUS'S* **LONG NECK,** compared

to **7** in almost all **MAMMALS,** including humans.

Only 5 near-complete to complete **CAMARASAURUS NECKS** have ever been found.

One of the **MOST-COMPLETE SAUROPOD SKELETONS** ever recovered is specimen **CM 11338**, a young *C. lentus* unearthed in **UTAH**, in **1909**.

Camarasaurus had a **BLUNT SKULL** with **CHISEL-LIKE TEETH** up to **4³/₅IN** (11.7cm) long.

Named in **1877**, *CAMARASAURUS* was one of **56** dinosaurs discovered by **EDWARD DRINKER COPE** during the **"Bone Wars,"** a **RUSH TO COLLECT FOSSILS** in the **US**.

FOSSILS of *CAMARASAURUS* are quite common—more than **530 specimens** have been discovered in **100** locations in the **WESTERN UNITED STATES** alone.

There are **4 POSSIBLE SPECIES** of *Camarasaurus*, all dating to the Late Jurassic. The earliest, *C. GRANDIS*, lived more than **150 MILLION YEARS AGO**.

The biggest **CAMARASAURID**, *C. supremus*, maxed out at **52 TONS**, about the same weight as **2 STONES** from **STONEHENGE**.

CAMARASAURUS
was a medium-sized **SAUROPOD** that measured up to **65FT** (20m) in length.

Incredible
ICHTHYOSAURS

These four-flippered marine reptiles lived from the Triassic to the Cretaceous, and their fossils have been found on all seven continents. They evolved from land reptiles and gave birth to live young. Ichthyosaurs had streamlined, dolphinlike bodies and a beak full of sharp teeth for hunting prey.

ICHTHYOSAURS RANGED IN SIZE from around

5FT
(1.5m) to over

82FT
(25m).

Ichthyosaur FRONT FLIPPERS contain digits like **FINGERS**, some with up to

30 BONES.

ICHTHYOSAUR FOSSILS have been found in rocks dating to **250—90 MILLION YEARS AGO**. There are more than

100
KNOWN SPECIES.

STENOPTERYGIUS could **SWIM** at speeds of up to **62MPH** (100kph).

The **LARGEST ICHTHYOSAUR TOOTH** was discovered in **2022**. The **INCOMPLETE CHOMPER** is **4IN** (10cm) long, with a root

2 times wider
than any previous find.

To see in the ocean's dark depths, *Temnodontosaurus* had eyes that were

12IN
(30cm) in diameter, **BIGGER THAN A BASKETBALL** and the **LARGEST OF ANY VERTEBRATE.**

The **SMALLEST ICHTHYOSAUR FOSSIL** of the type *I. communis* is a newborn. It was just

28IN

(70cm) long but already had the remains of a **SQUID DINNER** in its stomach.

The **first-KNOWN FOSSILS** that came from an **ICHTHYOSAUR** were recorded in a scientific illustration drawn in **WALES, UK,** in

1699.

An ichthyosaur fossil found in **CHINA** in **2010** shows that **ICHTHYOSAURS ATE OTHER LARGE MARINE REPTILES**–its

16FT-

(4.9m-) **LONG STOMACH** had a

13FT-

(4m-) **LONG THALATTOSAUR** inside!

The probable **OLDEST ICHTHYOSAUR FOSSIL** dates to about **250 million** YEARS AGO. The **UNNAMED SPECIMEN** was found in **SVALBARD, NORWAY,** in **2023.**

The tiny **16IN-** (0.4m-) long *Cartorhynchus lenticarpus* was a **SEAL-LIKE, EARLY ICHTHYOSAUR** that lived both in the **SEA** and on **LAND.**

An ichthyosaur fossil, dating to **160 MILLION YEARS AGO,** contains what some experts argue is the **OLDEST-KNOWN EXAMPLE OF VOMIT.** The specimen was full of **BELEMNITE** (squidlike shellfish) shells.

KRONOSAURUS

had an estimated **BITE FORCE** of

30,000 newtons, TWICE that of a SALTWATER CROCODILE.

PLESIOSAURS ranged from **6—56FT** (2-17m) in **LENGTH.**

A **KRONOSAURUS** skeleton uncovered in **AUSTRALIA** in **1932** was reconstructed at **HARVARD UNIVERSITY** with at least

7 VERTEBRAE TOO MANY.

A MASSIVE PLIOSAUR SKULL dating to the Late Jurassic was excavated **36FT** (11m) up an English cliffside in **2023.** It was **7FT** (1.7m) long with

130 teeth and a bite
capable of chomping through a car.

PLESIOSAUR FOSSIL REMAINS
have been unearthed on all

7 continents.

BITE MARKS found on the **SKULL** of an **EROMANGASAURUS** are probably from **ANOTHER PLESIOSAUR** that had **TEETH** up to

12IN
(30cm) long.

Spectacular
PLESIOSAURS

Ruling the seas from the Late Triassic through the Cretaceous, these four-flippered predators are commonly called "sea dragons." Plesiosaurs had long, snakelike necks and smaller heads, while closely related pliosaurs had short necks and crocodilelike jaws.

ALBERTONECTES VANDERVELDEI'S NECK was **SO LONG,** it made up **63%** of its **OVERALL LENGTH.**

The **LARGEST-KNOWN FOSSIL VERTEBRAE** from a **pliosaur** are around **10½IN** (27cm) across, as wide as **DINNER PLATES.**

Albertonectes vanderveldei had **76** **NECK VERTEBRAE**—the record for the **MOST** of **ANY ANIMAL IN HISTORY.**

PLESIOSAURS had **4 FLIPPERS.** Their **HIND PAIR** helped them **SWIM FASTER** by creating **60%** **MORE THRUST** in the water.

Some plesiosaurs were adapted to feed and **LIVE IN FRESH WATER.** Members of the **LEPTOCLEIDIDAE FAMILY** were recently found in a **100-MILLION-YEAR-OLD RIVER SYSTEM** in **MOROCCO.**

A PREGNANT *POLYCOTYLUS LATIPPINUS* fossil found in **KANSAS,** with a **FETUS** **5FT** (1.5m) long shows that plesiosaurs **GAVE BIRTH** to **LIVE YOUNG,** like mammals.

MARY ANNING'S SEA MONSTERS

Born in 1799, Mary Anning was one of the earliest and greatest fossil hunters and paleontologists, collecting specimens of ancient creatures that once swam in warm Jurassic seas from the coastal cliffs around her home in Lyme Regis, England. Her finds include some historic firsts.

With its long neck and **4 FLIPPERS,** Mary's **"SEA DRAGON"** *Plesiosaurus* looked so absurd that some scientists **THOUGHT IT WAS A HOAX.**

Mary **EXCAVATED AND PREPARED** the first specimen of the **GHOST SHARK** *Squaloraja* in **2 PIECES,** which she sold separately. Only the tail survived **WORLD WAR II BOMBINGS.**

In **2015,** the expert who helped make this book, Dr. Dean Lomax, co-named *ICHTHYOSAURUS ANNINGAE* **IN HONOR OF MARY.** She found **1** of the specimens used to make the identification.

LYME REGIS is part of the **Jurassic Coast,** a **95 mile** (150km) stretch of **FOSSIL-RICH COASTLINE,** with specimens spanning **185 million years** of Earth's history.

In **1828,** Mary uncovered a **"FLYING DRAGON"**—the first **pterodactyl** remains to be found outside **GERMANY.**

The **FIRST COMPLETE** plesiosaur skeleton was discovered by Mary in **1823.**

Mary helped identify **COPROLITES** (fossilized poo) for the first time in **1824**, including one that contained the **1IN** (2.5cm) vertebra of an **ICHTHYOSAUR.**

There is only **1 species** of *PLESIOSAURUS*, *P. DOLICHODEIRUS*, based on the **11FT 6IN** (3.5m) **FOSSIL SKELETON** Mary found.

Mary was only **12 YEARS OLD** when she and her brother Joseph found the **first ever ichthyosaur** to be studied scientifically.

This **ICHTHYOSAUR SKULL**, the first that Mary excavated, is more than **3FT 3IN** (1m) long.

R. 1158

200 MILLION YEARS AGO, the center of the **supercontinent Pangea** was flooded by a sea. Evidence of this is visible in the shale and limestone cliffs of Lyme Regis.

Mary made a living by selling her specimens. The **HIGHEST PRICE** she got for one was **200 GUINEAS** ($23,800 today) for a *PLESIOSAURUS MACROCEPHALUS*, now thought to be a young rhomaleosaurid plesiosaur, in **1830.**

Over **150 species** of pterosaur have been **IDENTIFIED BY SCIENTISTS**, from the **CROW-SIZED** *EUDIMORPHODON* to the **GLIDER-SIZED** *QUETZALCOATLUS NORTHROPI*.

PTEROSAURS were the **EARLIEST VERTEBRATES** (animals with backbones) to have **EVOLVED** into **FLYING CREATURES**. *Eudimorphodon* launched into the air more than **219 MILLION YEARS AGO.**

The **LARGEST** of the **PTEROSAURS**, *QUETZALCOATLUS NORTHROPI* weighed less than **550LB** (250kg) due to its **HOLLOW BONES.**

The **CRESTS** of **PTEROSAURS** came in many shapes and sizes. *NYCTOSAURUS* had a **22IN-** (55cm-) tall **DOUBLE-PRONGED CREST,** but its **BODY** was only **15IN** (37cm) tall.

Studies of **FOOTPRINTS** show pterosaurs **WALKED ON ALL**  **4 LIMBS,** with their wings **FOLDED BACKWARD.**

EUDIMORPHODON had **110 SHARP TEETH** **PACKED** into a **JAW** as **SHORT** as a **HUMAN FINGER.**

Terrific
PTEROSAURS

These flying reptiles soared above waters and coastlines around the world at the time of the dinosaurs, from the Late Triassic to the Late Cretaceous. Most ate fish, scooping them up from rivers and seas. Inland pterosaurs may have hunted insects and reptiles, too.

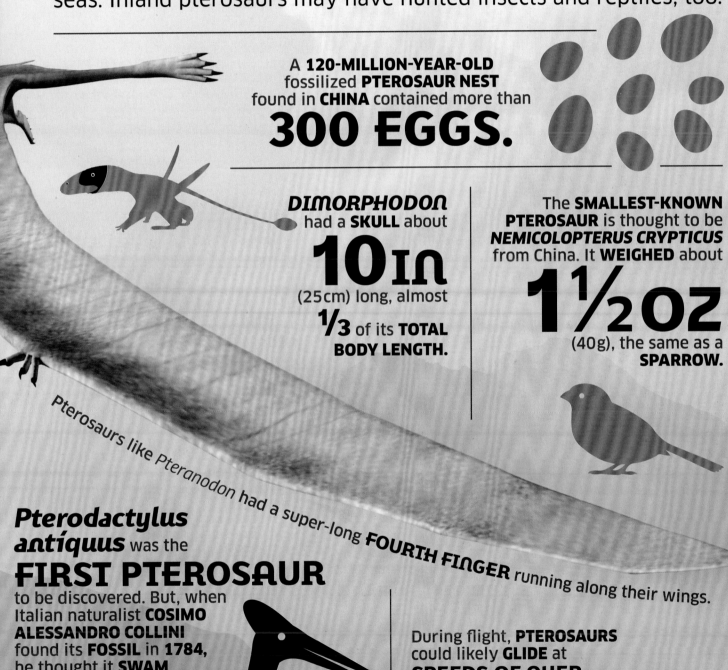

A **120-MILLION-YEAR-OLD** fossilized **PTEROSAUR NEST** found in **CHINA** contained more than
300 EGGS.

DIMORPHODON had a **SKULL** about
10IN
(25cm) long, almost **1/3** of its **TOTAL BODY LENGTH.**

The **SMALLEST-KNOWN PTEROSAUR** is thought to be **NEMICOLOPTERUS CRYPTICUS** from China. It **WEIGHED** about
1½OZ
(40g), the same as a **SPARROW.**

Pterosaurs like Pteranodon had a super-long **FOURTH FINGER** running along their wings.

Pterodactylus antiquus was the
FIRST PTEROSAUR
to be discovered. But, when Italian naturalist **COSIMO ALESSANDRO COLLINI** found its **FOSSIL** in 1784, he thought it **SWAM** instead of flew.

During flight, **PTEROSAURS** could likely **GLIDE** at **SPEEDS OF OVER**
75MPH (120kph).

Sky-high
DIPLODOCIDS

Dinosaurs such as *Diplodocus*, *Apatosaurus*, and *Barosaurus* were all diplodocids—giant four-legged, plant-eating sauropods from the Late Jurassic Period. They had long necks and whiplike tails. Their back legs were longer than their front pair, which may have allowed them to rear up to feed from high branches.

DIPLODOCIDS DISAPPEARED in the **EARLY CRETACEOUS PERIOD**, around **136 million years ago.**

APATOSAURUS had the **CAPACITY** for **110 gallons** (500 liters) of **BLOOD** in its **HEART.** Its **LUNGS** could have held **240 GALLONS** (900 liters) of **AIR.**

Diplodocids had about **40 PEGLIKE TEETH,** which they used to **STRIP TREES** of **LEAVES.**

Diplodocus fossils were **FIRST DISCOVERED** in **1877.**

Dippy, the **FAMOUS DIPLODOCUS** skeleton given to London's **NATURAL HISTORY MUSEUM** in **1905**, is one of **11 casts** of the **ORIGINAL SKELETON** displayed around the world.

Measuring 82ft (25m), DIPLODOCUS is the LONGEST DINOSAUR KNOWN FROM A COMPLETE SKELETON.

A **DIPLODOCUS NECK** contained **15 VERTEBRAE,** while its **TAIL HAD 80.** Its tail may have been **USED LIKE A WHIP** for **DEFENSE.**

Despite its huge size, **DIPLODOCUS** had a **TINY BRAIN, 150,000 TIMES LESS** than its **BODY WEIGHT.** It **WEIGHED** an estimated **4 OZ** (114g), which is more than **12 TIMES LESS** than the weight of an **ADULT HUMAN BRAIN.**

At up to **30 FT** (9m) **LONG,** *Barosaurus's* **neck** was **3 TIMES** the length of an **ADULT GIRAFFE'S.**

FAST-GROWING DIPLODOCUS only took an estimated **10 YEARS** to reach **ADULTHOOD** and may have **LIVED** for up to **100 YEARS.**

An **ADULT** *Apatosaurus* **WEIGHED** up to **22 tons,** as **HEAVY** as **10 hippos.**

Diplodocus's name comes from **2 GREEK WORDS,** **"DIPLOS"** and **"DOKOS,"** meaning **"DOUBLE BEAM,"** which is a nod to its **ARROW-SHAPED** tail bones.

DIPLODOCIDS are thought to have traveled in **HERDS** like **CATTLE,** in groups numbering up to **30 individuals.**

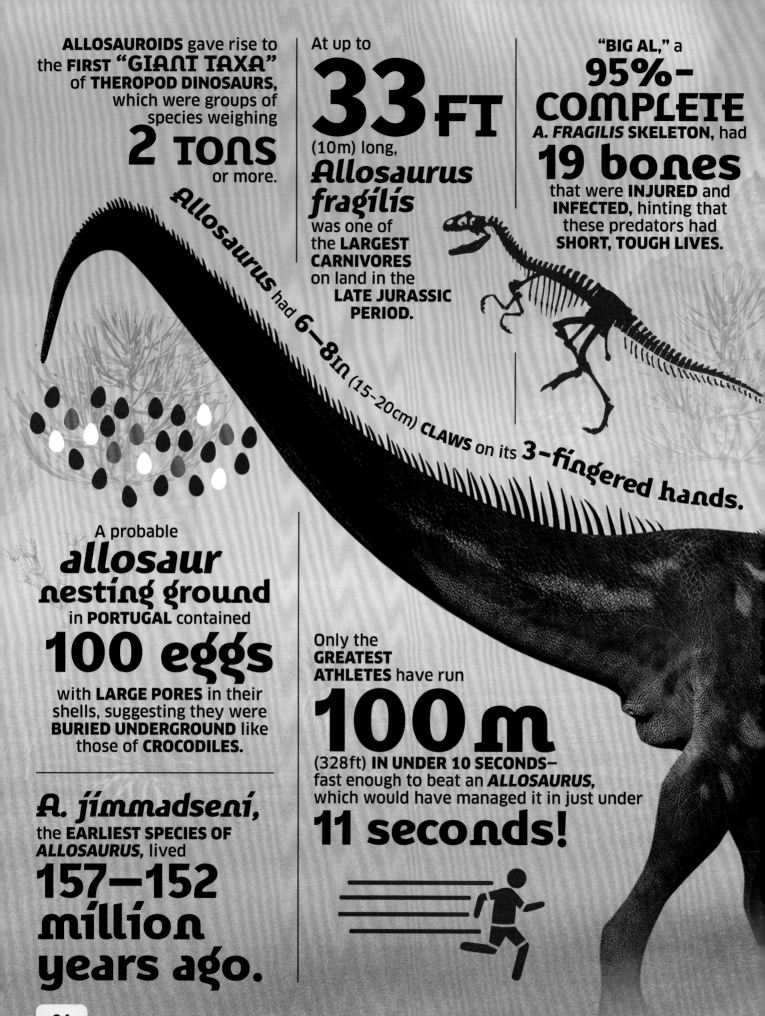

ALLOSAUROIDS gave rise to the **FIRST "GIANT TAXA"** of **THEROPOD DINOSAURS**, which were groups of species weighing **2 TONS** or more.

At up to **33 FT** (10m) long, *Allosaurus fragilis* was one of the **LARGEST CARNIVORES** on land in the **LATE JURASSIC PERIOD**.

"BIG AL," a **95%–COMPLETE** *A. FRAGILIS* SKELETON, had **19 bones** that were **INJURED** and **INFECTED**, hinting that these predators had **SHORT, TOUGH LIVES**.

Allosaurus had **6—8 IN** (15–20cm) **CLAWS** on its **3-fingered hands.**

A probable **allosaur nesting ground** in **PORTUGAL** contained **100 eggs** with **LARGE PORES** in their shells, suggesting they were **BURIED UNDERGROUND** like those of **CROCODILES**.

Only the **GREATEST ATHLETES** have run **100 m** (328ft) **IN UNDER 10 SECONDS**— fast enough to beat an *ALLOSAURUS*, which would have managed it in just under **11 seconds!**

A. jimmadseni, the **EARLIEST SPECIES OF** *ALLOSAURUS*, lived **157—152 million years ago.**

Aggressive ALLOSAURS

For around 10 million years in the Late Jurassic, the long-legged, three-toed theropod *Allosaurus* was a common and deadly predator. Unlike later tyrannosaurs, its arms were long and strong enough to hold its prey, which it chased or ambushed.

Allosaurus's small and light **SKULL** had **2 SHORT HORNS** with **RIDGES** running from its **EYES TO ITS NOSTRILS.**

ALLOSAUROID relatives of ***ALLOSAURUS*** were among the **BIGGEST PREDATORS** on Earth for **85 million years.**

Allosaurus had **2–4IN-** (5–10cm-) long, **KNIFELIKE TEETH** that **CURVED BACKWARD,** perfect for **HOLDING AND SLICING ITS PREY.**

The **FIRST *A. jimmadseni*** specimen was found in **1990.** The bones were **RADIOACTIVE,** so its **MISSING SKULL** was located **6 years** later using a **RADIATION DETECTOR.**

A **2¼IN** (5.7cm) **bite mark** in a **STEGOSAURUS NECK PLATE** shows it was **HUNTED** by an ***ALLOSAURUS,*** while a **1½IN-** (4cm-) **WIDE HOLE** in an ***ALLOSAURUS* VERTEBRA** shows it was **ATTACKED** by a ***STEGOSAURUS* SPIKE.**

Iconic
ARCHAEOPTERYX

Is it a bird? Is it a dinosaur? *Archaeopteryx* has been called both! After the first skeleton—one of the most famous fossils of all time—was discovered in the 19th century, many experts described it as an ancient bird. Today, the debate goes on as to whether it's the earliest true bird or birdlike relative that could fly or glide.

The **FIRST *ARCHAEOPTERYX* SKELETON** was found in **1861,** with **IMPRESSIVE FEATHERS** visible on its **TAIL AND WINGS.**

Archaeopteryx **HATCHLINGS** took almost **3 YEARS TO MATURE** to adulthood, at least **3 TIMES** longer than **MODERN BIRDS** of the **SAME SIZE.**

Modern technology has revealed the **COLOR OF**

1

ARCHAEOPTERYX feather—it was **jet black,** but it's **NOT KNOWN** if the animal was the **SAME COLOR ALL OVER.**

Unlike modern birds, *Archaeopteryx* had a mouth full of **50 CONE-SHAPED TEETH,** ideal for **CHOMPING** on **SMALL PREY,** such as lizards and insects.

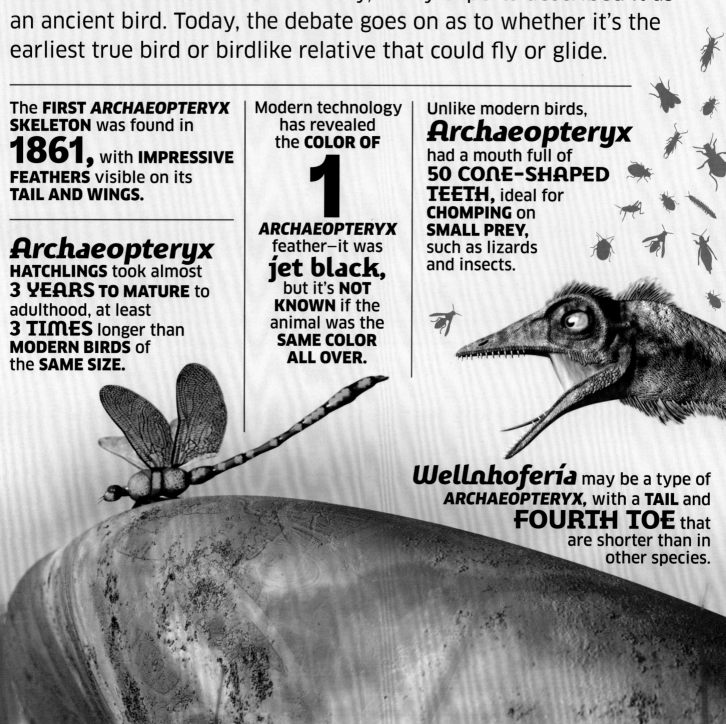

Wellnhoferia may be a type of **ARCHAEOPTERYX,** with a **TAIL** and **FOURTH TOE** that are shorter than in other species.

An **Archaeopteryx lithographica** fossil has been dated at **153 million years old.** Some scientists have argued it is the **EARLIEST FLYING BIRD.**

To celebrate the **150TH ANNIVERSARY** of the **FIRST ARCHAEOPTERYX FOSSIL** being found, a special **10-euro coin** was issued in **GERMANY in 2011.**

ARCHAEOPTERYX had **2 feathered wings LIKE A BIRD** and **1 long, bony tail LIKE A DINOSAUR.** No living animal combines these **2 features.**

The **3 CLAWED DIGITS** on each of *Archaeopteryx's* **WINGS** were likely used to **CLIMB TREES** and **CLUTCH BRANCHES.**

Weighing around **2LB 3OZ** (1kg), **ARCHAEOPTERYX** would probably have been able to **FLY SHORT DISTANCES** to **EVADE PREDATORS.**

A total of **12 Archaeopteryx** specimens have been found –**ALL** in or nearby **SOLNHOFEN, GERMANY.**

ARCHAEOPTERYX had **1 RAISED CLAW** on the **second TOE** of each foot. Known as **"killing claws,"** they could be used to lash out at an **ATTACKER.**

ARCHAEOPTERYX was **20IN** (50cm) long–about the same size as a **PIGEON.**

BRACHIOSAURUS needed a **BIG STOMACH** to digest about **400LB** (880kg) of leaves every day, the equivalent of about

480 cabbages.

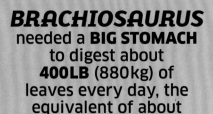

Brachiosaurus was given its name, meaning **"arm lizard,"** because its **FRONT LEGS** were

2 FT

(60cm) **LONGER THAN ITS BACK LEGS.**

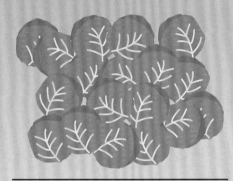

To **PUMP BLOOD** up its **28 FT-** (8.5m-) long neck to its head, a *Brachiosaurus* would have needed a **POWERFUL HEART,** perhaps weighing

880 LB

(400kg), as heavy as a **GRAND PIANO.**

GASTROLITHS are stones that help animals digest **TOUGH PLANT MATTER.** A *Cedarosaurus* specimen was found with

115 gastroliths

weighing **15LB** (7kg) in its **STOMACH.**

BRACHIOSAURUS had

26 teeth

clustered at the front of both its **UPPER AND LOWER JAWS** for stripping vegetation.

Most of the vertebrae in a **BRACHIOSAURUS** neck were

3 FT 3 IN

(1m) long,

30 times

longer than a **HUMAN NECK BONE.**

The world's **TALLEST MOUNTED DINOSAUR SKELETON** on display is a

43 FT 6 IN

(13.3m) *GIRAFFATITAN* from Tanzania.

Brilliant
BRACHIOSAURS

These long-necked herbivores roamed around much of the planet in the Late Jurassic, shearing through plants with their thick, chisel-shaped teeth. Brachiosaurids, such as *Brachiosaurus* and *Giraffatitan*, had long front legs and, unlike most other sauropods, were able to keep their heads and necks upright.

Portugal's **150-MILLION-YEAR-OLD** *LUSOTITAN* was originally named *BRACHIOSAURUS ATALAIENSIS* in 1957, before being designated as its **OWN GENUS** **46 years** later.

Europasaurus, a **COW-SIZED BRACHIOSAURID** that was isolated on an island, evolved to be **RELATIVELY SMALL.** At **20 FT** (6.2m), it was **1/4** the length of **BRACHIOSAURUS.**

A CT scan of a *Giraffatitan* **JAW** revealed **2 REPLACEMENT TEETH** behind each tooth that was in use, suggesting they could have been **REPLACED** as often as every **64 days.**

Unlike most other sauropods, Brachiosaurus is thought to have kept its head at **45 DEGREES**, like a **GIRAFFE.**

An adult *Brachiosaurus* thigh bone was as tall as an **ADULT HUMAN**, around **6 FT** (1.8m).

TOP 5
SMALLEST
DINOSAURS

Not all dinosaurs were towering giants. While the tiniest ever dino is technically today's bee hummingbird, the Mesozoic Age of the Dinosaurs saw some fairly small species, too.

ANCHIORNIS HUXLEYI
Late Jurassic • **SHANDONG, CHINA**
Weight: **4OZ** (110g)

1

Only 24in (60cm) long, the tiny theropod *Anchiornis* was covered with feathers from its crested head to its plumed feet. Hundreds of well-preserved fossils from 160 million years ago have revealed this "near bird" in great detail.

2 ### MAHAKALA OMNOGOVAE
Late Cretaceous • **ÖMNÖGOVI, MONGOLIA**
Weight: **25OZ** (700g)

A partial skeleton of this small, 75-million-year-old species named after a Buddhist protector deity was found in the Gobi desert. A dromaeosaurid measuring 28in (70cm) in length, *Mahakala* is seen as evidence of how dinosaurs grew smaller as they evolved into flying birds.

3 ### MICRORAPTOR GUI
Early Cretaceous • **LIAONING, CHINA**
Weight: **2LB** (1kg)

Remarkable fossils of this crow-sized dromaeosaurid dinosaur dating to 120 million years ago indicate that it had black, iridescent feathers similar to a magpie's. Just 30in (77cm) long, *Microraptor* had not two wings but four!

4 ### AQUILOPS AMERICANUS
Early Cretaceous • **MONTANA, US**
Weight: **3LB** (1.5kg)

Estimated to be 24in (60cm) in length, this early ancestor of *Triceratops* was up to 40,000 times smaller than its massive relative. The bunny-sized species—named "eagle face" for its beaked skull—was found in rocks dating to 106 million years ago.

5 ### MICROPACHYCEPHALOSAURUS HONGTUYANENSIS
Late Cretaceous • **SHANDONG, CHINA** • Weight: **3LB** (1.5kg)

This ceratopsian may boast the longest name of any dinosaur, but it was genuinely tiny at an estimated 24in (60cm) long. Unearthed in 1972 in China, this rare specimen may be a young example of a bigger dome-headed dinosaur.

Super finds
LIAONING FEATHERS

For more than 160 years, scientists have speculated that dinosaurs and birds were related. In the last 30 years, discoveries of fossilized feathers from northeastern China's Liaoning province have allowed them to confirm the connection in exquisite, colorful detail. They also show how feathers evolved to help dinosaurs take flight.

The **earliest dinosaur feathers,** like those from the downy, **1/10IN** (3mm) **COAT** of *SINOSAUROPTERYX,* were for **INSULATION.**

Dating to **160 MILLION YEARS AGO,** *ANCHIORNIS* was **10 million years older** than what was once thought of as the **"FIRST BIRD,"** *ARCHAEOPTERYX.*

Yutyrannus, the **LARGEST-KNOWN FEATHERED ANIMAL,** at **1.5 tons,** had **INSULATING FEATHERS ALL OVER ITS BODY.**

MANY LIAONING FEATHERS are from the **Jehol Biota,** an **EARLY CRETACEOUS ECOSYSTEM** finely preserved under **VOLCANIC ASH** from an eruption **130 MILLION YEARS AGO.**

Discovered in 2009, *ANCHIORNIS* is the earliest dinosaur with flight feathers. It had **4 WINGS.**

Liaoning has yielded **6 TYPES** of **FEATHERY DROMAEOSAURID DINOSAUR.** The **LARGEST,** *Tianyuraptor* and *Zhenyuanlong,* had **STRANGELY SHORT WINGS** just **1/2 THE LENGTH OF THEIR LEGS.**

A very detailed specimen of one of the earliest-known toothless birds, the **10IN-** (25cm-) long ***Confuciusornis,*** revealed that it had **SPOTS** on its **THROAT, WINGS,** and **CREST** for camouflage and display.

The iridescent bird ***EOCONFUCIUSORNIS*** had **2 STREAMERLIKE TAIL FEATHERS** displayed to attract mates.

Scientists drew upon over **100 FEATHERY *Microraptor*** specimens to develop a **FLIGHT MODEL** that suggests it could glide at a speed of **35FT PER SECOND** (10.6m per second).

Liaoning's **first FOSSIL MELANOSOMES** (the color-holding structures in feathers) were uncovered in **2010.**

SINORNITHOSAURUS **HAD 3 TYPES OF FEATHERS:** hairy fibers, sprays, and stiff, asymmetrical plumes **LIKE** those of **MODERN BIRDS.**

DILONG, the **EARLIEST TYRANNOSAUR** with **EVIDENCE OF FEATHERS,** had filaments (hairlike structures) ⁴/₅IN (2cm) in length.

Compsognathus longipes—discovered in Bavaria, Germany, **IN THE 1850s**—was the **FIRST** NEAR-COMPLETE **THEROPOD SKELETON** unearthed.

A **130-million-year-old** *SINOSAUROPTERYX* was the **FIRST DINOSAUR** to have its **FEATHER COLOR DECODED**—red-brown with orange and white bands.

Only **1 Jurassic dinosaur fossil** has been found in **NEW ZEALAND**—a **150-MILLION-YEAR-OLD COMPSOGNATHID PHALANX** (finger bone).

COMPSOGNATHUS was only **4FT 3IN** (1.3m) long and about **6LB** (2.5kg), roughly the **SIZE** and **WEIGHT** of a **CHICKEN.**

SINOSAUROPTERYX could lay **2 eggs** at a time, which it would incubate until they hatched.

SCIPIONYX was the **FIRST DINOSAUR FOUND IN ITALY.** Thought to be just **3 weeks old,** the specimen measured **20IN** (50cm) long.

The **LARGEST COMPSOGNATHID** is *Sinocalliopteryx,* meaning **"CHINESE BEAUTIFUL FEATHER."** It may have reached **8FT** (2.4m) long.

Compsognathus had **3 FINGERS,** but the **THIRD** was much smaller than the other 2.

Tiny COMPSOGNATHIDS

Found in South America, Europe, and Asia, compsognathids are among the smallest dinosaurs, and some had feathers. These petite meat-eaters from the Jurassic and Cretaceous Periods ran on two legs and hunted insects and small lizards.

Compsognathus was a **SCAVENGER** and **HUNTER** with about **40** **NEEDLE-SHARP TEETH.**

The **LARGEST** *SINOSAUROPTERYX* was **3 FT 3 IN** (1m) from **JAWS TO TIP OF TAIL** and may have **WEIGHED** just **2 LB 3 OZ** (1kg)— the **SAME** as an **AVERAGE PINEAPPLE.**

An early **CRETACEOUS COMPSOGNATHID,** *Sinosauropteryx,* found in China in **1996,** was the **first fossil** of a **NONFLYING DINOSAUR** to show signs of **FEATHERS.**

SINOSAUROPTERYX had **64 bones** in its super-long, **WHIPLIKE TAIL.**

The **SIMPLE, BRISTLY FEATHERS** on *SINOSAUROPTERYX* were **LONGEST** on its **TAIL,** measuring up to **1³/₅ IN** (4cm) in length.

CRETACEOUS

The **CRETACEOUS PERIOD** lasted from
145 to 66 million years ago.

Spanning **79 MILLION YEARS**, the Cretaceous was the

third,
FINAL, AND LONGEST PERIOD of the **MESOZOIC ERA** of the dinosaurs.

The **30FT-** (9m-) long **YUTYRANNUS** was the **TOP PREDATOR** of the dinos found in China's Cretaceous Yixian Formation.

SEA-SURFACE TEMPERATURES during the **CRETACEOUS** reached
79–95°F
(26–35°C).

The name **CRETACEOUS** comes from the **LATIN WORD** for **"CHALK"** because layers of the rock chalk—up to
5,000FT
(1,500m) thick in the **NORTH SEA**—were deposited during the period.

SEA LEVELS were up to
656FT
(200m) **HIGHER THAN TODAY.**

CRETACEOUS WORLD

During the 79 million years of the Cretaceous Period, the continents we know today began to form as the Atlantic Ocean widened and flooded inland to create warm, shallow seas. Dinosaurs and other reptiles remained the dominant species, but their rule was to come to an untimely end.

FLOWERING PLANTS now make up about **90%** of all plants. They **FIRST BECAME WIDESPREAD** during the **CRETACEOUS** and included species of *MAGNOLIA*, *FICUS*, and *SASSAFRAS*.

BEES evolved from wasps over **120 million years ago**, when they **BEGAN POLLINATING** some flowers.

Broad-leaved trees, including **OAK, BEECH, AND MAPLE**, began to replace **CYCADS AND CONIFERS** in forests **140 to 100 million years ago.**

NORTHERN HEMISPHERE dinosaurs reached their **BIGGEST SIZE** during the Jurassic, while those of the **SOUTHERN HEMISPHERE** peaked in the **CRETACEOUS**, with **titanosaurs** up to **70 TONS.**

ICE-FREE ANTARCTICA was home to *Vegavis*, a **12 IN-** (30cm-) long **DIVING BIRD** that looked and honked **LIKE A goose.**

CRETACEOUS soil samples from **ANTARCTICA** show that the **SOUTH POLE** was covered in **TEMPERATE RAINFOREST** even though there was **no sunlight** for **1/3** of the year.

A tiny, **9IN-** (23cm-) long **Camptosaurus** SPECIMEN was found to be an **UNHATCHED EMBRYO**, even though its shell was not preserved.

The name *IGUANODON* means "IGUANA TEETH." It had **SIMILAR TEETH** to the living **IGUANA** but about **20 TIMES LARGER.**

In **15 sites,** remains of plant-eating *Tenotosaurus* have been found alongside those of meat-eating **DEINONYCHUS,** suggesting the **IGUANODONT** was one of its **FAVORITE FOODS.**

Iguanodon had **5 FINGERS** on each hand, including **3 MIDDLE FINGERS** that were partly **FUSED TOGETHER** and a **6IN-** (14cm-) long **THUMB SPIKE.**

Iguanodon was the **second-ever** DINOSAUR to be named.

NIGER'S strangely stout **LURDUSAURUS** was **30FT** (9m) **LONG** with a **MASSIVE BELLY** that hung only **28IN** (70cm) **ABOVE THE GROUND.**

The **OLDEST-DATED BIOLOGICAL MOLECULES** belong to an *Iguanodon.* They were taken from a **FOSSILIZED RIB** found in the **UK** and date to **125 MILLION YEARS AGO.**

Intriguing
IGUANODONTS

One of the very first dinosaurs identified, *Iguanodon* was a large plant-eater from the Early Cretaceous known for its distinctive thumb spike. There were many types of iguanodont, which were beaked, five-fingered herbivores that walked on four legs but could rise onto their back ones to pluck leaves from trees.

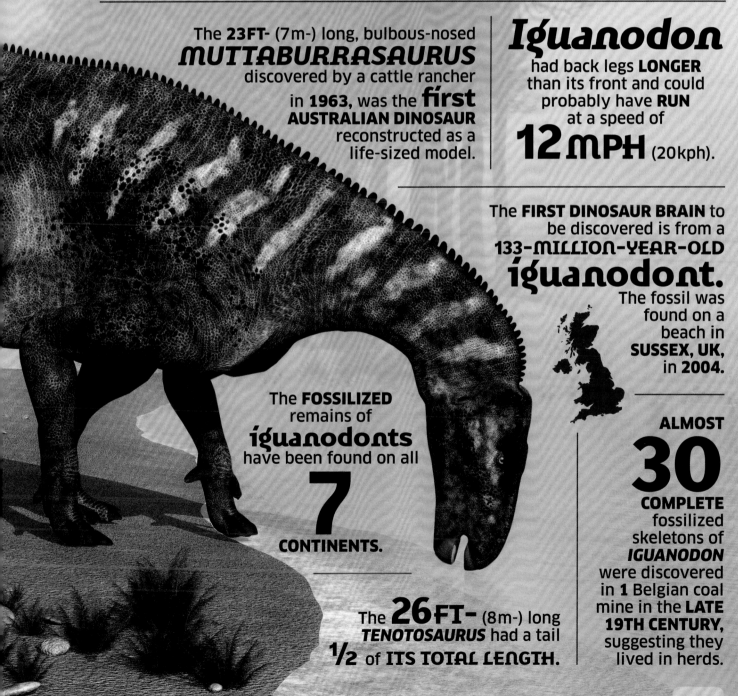

The **23FT-** (7m-) long, bulbous-nosed **MUTTABURRASAURUS** discovered by a cattle rancher in **1963**, was the **first AUSTRALIAN DINOSAUR** reconstructed as a life-sized model.

Iguanodon
had back legs **LONGER** than its front and could probably have **RUN** at a speed of **12 MPH** (20kph).

The **FIRST DINOSAUR BRAIN** to be discovered is from a **133-MILLION-YEAR-OLD iguanodont.** The fossil was found on a beach in **SUSSEX, UK,** in **2004**.

The **FOSSILIZED** remains of **iguanodonts** have been found on all **7 CONTINENTS.**

ALMOST 30 COMPLETE fossilized skeletons of **IGUANODON** were discovered in **1** Belgian coal mine in the **LATE 19TH CENTURY**, suggesting they lived in herds.

The **26 FT-** (8m-) long **TENOTOSAURUS** had a tail **½** of **ITS TOTAL LENGTH.**

Savage
SPINOSAURIDS

Monster fish lived during the Cretaceous Period–and so did monster-sized fish hunters, like the long-snouted spinosaurids. As well as snaring prey in the water, these huge carnivorous dinosaurs were skilled at catching creatures on land.

A SPINOSAURID had
2 NOSTRILS
CLOSER TO ITS EYES than to the **TIP OF ITS SNOUT.** This allowed it to breathe when trying to **CATCH PREY IN THE WATER.**

In 2021, **2 new species** of spinosaurids were discovered on the Isle of Wight, UK: *CERATOSUCHOPS INFERODIOS* and *RIPAROVENATOR MILNERAE.*

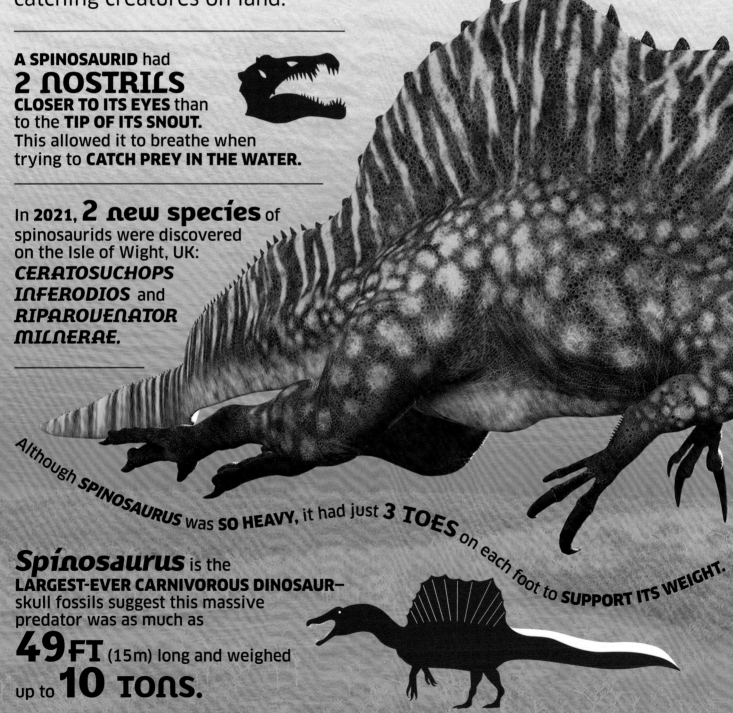

Although **SPINOSAURUS** was **SO HEAVY**, it had just **3 TOES** on each foot to **SUPPORT ITS WEIGHT.**

Spinosaurus is the **LARGEST-EVER CARNIVOROUS DINOSAUR–** skull fossils suggest this massive predator was as much as
49FT (15m) long and weighed
up to **10 TONS.**

Many of the best **Spinosaurus** fossils were destroyed by bombs that hit a museum in **MUNICH, GERMANY,** during **WORLD WAR II.**

A **Spinosaurus's** SAIL was supported by **SPINES** at least **5 FT** (1.6m) long, although some scientists think it might have had a **HUMP ON ITS BACK** instead.

The **FIRST SPINOSAURUS** was discovered **IN EGYPT IN 1915,** but it took **99 years** for **ANOTHER LARGE SET** of fossils to be **DISCOVERED.**

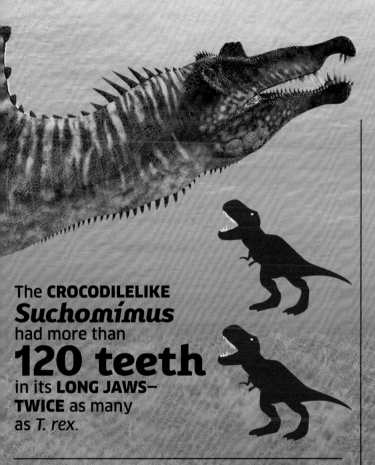

The **LARGEST ANIMATRONIC MODEL** ever made for a **MOVIE** was the **44 FT-** (13.4m-) long **SPINOSAURUS** built for **JURASSIC PARK III.**

Baryonyx had a large, **12 IN-** (30cm-) long **CLAW-BONE** on each hand, perfect for **SPEARING FISH.**

The **CROCODILELIKE Suchomimus** had more than **120 teeth** in its **LONG JAWS—TWICE** as many as *T. rex.*

More than **16 TONS** of **ROCK AND SAND** had to be **MOVED** to dig up a **Suchomimus** skeleton in the **SAHARA** in 1997.

The **26 FT-** (8m-) **LONG Irritator** was so named because paleontologists were **IRRITATED BY DAMAGE** to its fossilized skull, which had been altered with **car body filler.**

Scans of the **SKULLS** of **2** of the oldest spinosaurids, **BARYONYX** and **CERATOSUCHOPS,** showed that their teeth and snouts adapted to their semi-aquatic lifestyles before their brains did.

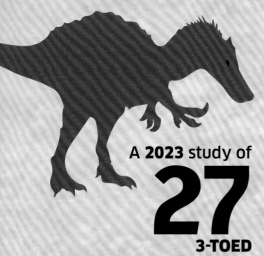

A **2023** study of

27

3-TOED FOOTPRINTS found they were made by a **SWIMMING SPINOSAURID.**

There may be **AS MANY AS**

70,000

FOOTPRINTS across La Rioja.

In a **GREAT EXAMPLE** of a **CITIZEN SCIENCE PROJECT,** students and other local residents have led the way in **MAPPING FOOTPRINTS** in the region, which has

170

PALEONTOLOGICAL SITES.

With **IMPRINTS** up to

8IN (20cm)

deep, the **TRACKWAYS** of La Rioja are **"TRACE FOSSILS,"** a **RECORD OF ANIMAL ACTIVITY RATHER THAN** the **REMAINS** of the animal itself.

The **PRINTS** belong to

3 kinds

of dinosaurs: **THEROPODS, ORNITHOPODS,** and **SAUROPODS.**

NOBODY REALIZED the footprints belonged to **DINOSAURS** until

1969

when they were noticed by **2 SCIENTISTS** doing unrelated field work.

SPAIN is also home to many **EARLY CRETACEOUS** dinosaur remains–

15 types

were discovered at **1 SITE IN TERUEL.**

LA RIOJA FOOTPRINTS

In one region of northern Spain, there are thousands of ichnites (fossil footprints) visible in the Early Cretaceous rock. Now known to be the trackways of dinosaurs crossing ancient mudflats, these traces hold vital clues about dinosaur size, speed, behavior, and habitat.

LA RIOJA'S largest **SAUROPOD FOOTPRINT** is **30 BY 29IN** (76 by 73cm)— as big as a **STOP SIGN**.

STOP

Around **11,000 FOOTPRINTS** have been found **SO FAR.**

SIX FOOTPRINTS spaced **8FT 8IN** (2.65m) apart show the dino that made them was **RUNNING** at **28MPH** (45kph)— a new **SPEED RECORD FOR A LARGE THEROPOD!**

THEROPOD footprints are the **MOST COMMON,** making up more than **866** of the trackways identified.

One outcrop of limestone with **212** overlapping **ORNITHOPOD FOOTPRINTS** heading in the same direction shows that they **TRAVELED IN HERDS.**

The **FOOTPRINTS** date to the **EARLY CRETACEOUS,** around **120 million years ago.**

Duck-billed
HADROSAURS

These large plant-eaters had ducklike bills for clipping vegetation. Hadrosaurs lived during the Cretaceous, 90–66 million years ago. Many of them had amazing head crests, which might have been used to attract mates, regulate body temperature, or make loud calls.

Shantungosaurus is the **LARGEST-KNOWN HADROSAUR.** At a whopping **16 TONS,** it was about the **SAME WEIGHT** as **24 COWS.**

There are **3 known species** of the **"HOOKED-BEAKED LIZARD,"** *GRYPOSAURUS,* identified by its distinctive arched snout.

A 3-D model of *PARASAUROLOPHUS'S* hollow crest found it made trombonelike sounds.

The **SMALLEST, YOUNGEST FOSSIL SKELETON** of a *PARASAUROLOPHUS,* dating back to **75 million years ago,** was discovered by a **17-YEAR-OLD STUDENT.**

MAIASAURA laid batches of **20—40 eggs,** the **SAME SIZE AS OSTRICH EGGS.** Unlike many dinosaurs, they **CARED FOR THEIR BABIES** until they learned to walk.

A **HADROSAUR VERTEBRA** discovered in **2014** on Axel Heiberg Island, just

750 miles

(1,200km) from the North Pole, is the **northernmost dinosaur fossil ever found,** showing they lived even in Arctic regions!

The **FIRST DINOSAUR SKELETON EXHIBITED IN A MUSEUM** was *Hadrosaurus foulkii* in **1868** at the **ACADEMY OF NATURAL SCIENCES** in Philadelphia.

***PARASAUROLOPHUS'S* HEAD CREST** was up to

6 FT

(1.8m) long—**DOUBLE** the length of its skull.

Edmontosaurus likely had **THE MOST TEETH** of any dinosaur— with **MORE THAN**

1,000

DIAMOND-SHAPED CHOMPERS in its cheeks.

Studies of an ***EDMONTOSAURUS*** fossil nicknamed **"DAKOTA"** found it could probably run at

45 MPH

(28kph).

Olorotitan's name means **"GIGANTIC SWAN,"** because of its **LONG NECK,** which contained

18 vertebrae.

Humans and giraffes each have **7 NECK BONES.**

A hadrosaur was the **FIRST DINOSAUR IN SPACE**—fossils from a

76-million-year-old

MAIASAURA PEEBLESORUM flew on board ***SPACELAB 2*** in **1985.**

Beaked
PSITTACOSAURS

These petite plant-eating dinosaurs from Early Cretaceous Asia were early ceratopsians with horny growths on their cheeks. The name *Psittacosaurus* means "parrot lizard," a nod to their bony beaks. Scientists have found hundreds of very well preserved specimens, from eggs to adults, so we know more about them than most dinos.

Psittacosaurus could measure up to **6FT 6IN** (2m) in length and weigh up to **88LB** (40kg).

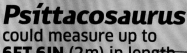

PSITTACOSAURUS had about **100**
6IN- (15cm-)
long **TAIL FILAMENTS.**

Over **1,000** PSITTACOSAUR SPECIMENS have been found, many with COMPLETE SKELETONS.

Up to **14 species** of *PSITTACOSAURUS* have been identified in **China, Mongolia, Russia,** and **Thailand.**

A **FOSSILIZED NEST of 34** young *PSITTACOSAURUS* was found in **2004,** suggesting **INFANTS** were looked after in **NURSERIES.**

The **first** *Psittacosaurus* REMAINS were discovered in **MONGOLIA** in **1923.**

Psittacosaurus was a nippy dinosaur **CAPABLE OF RUNNING** at **20.5 MPH** (33kph).

The **SMALLEST** fossilized remains of *Psittacosaurus* are those of **NEWLY HATCHED YOUNG** that were **10 IN** (26cm) long.

With **FRONT LIMBS 58%** the length of its **BACK LIMBS**, *PSITTACOSAURUS* was likely to have **WALKED ON 2 legs.**

The **LARGEST** of the species, *Psittacosaurus sibiricus,* had a **SKULL 8¼ IN** (20.7cm) long, the **LENGTH** of a **BRICK.**

The **oldest belly button** ever discovered is on a **125-MILLION-YEAR-OLD** fossilized *PSITTACOSAURUS.* It's a scar from where the **EMBRYO** was attached to the **EGG'S YOLK SAC.**

An adult **PSITTACOSAURUS** could live to age **10** or **11**.

In **2005,** the remains of a young *Psittacosaurus* were found in the gut of a **3FT 3IN-** (1m-) long *Repenomamus,* making it the **FIRST EXAMPLE OF A MAMMAL EATING A DINOSAUR!**

In **2016,** a team from the UK unveiled the **MOST ACCURATE 3-D model OF A DINOSAUR** to date, reconstructed using a *PSITTACOSAURUS MONGOLIENSIS* specimen complete with **SCALY BROWN SKIN.**

Sinornithosaurus millenii, found in **LIAONING, CHINA,** in **2001,** was the most **COMPLETE FEATHERED FOSSIL** ever discovered. The **2 FT-** (60 cm-) long **DUCK-SIZED** dinosaur was estimated to be **125 MILLION YEARS OLD.**

Fierce **DEINONYCHUS** ("terrible claw") had about **70 DAGGERLIKE SERRATED TEETH.**

While **Velociraptor** has appeared in movies as a human-sized **PREDATOR,** it was actually **7 FT** (2 m) long from **NOSE** to **TAIL,** but **SHORTER THAN A TURKEY.**

The raptor **DINEOBELLATOR** was named in **2020** and dates to **67 MILLION YEARS AGO.**

In **2001,** paleontologists working in **UTAH** recovered a **125-MILLION-YEAR-OLD, 9-ton "MEGABLOCK"** of sandstone filled with **FOSSILS,** including **DOZENS** of **Utahraptors** trapped in **QUICKSAND.**

The **CROW-SIZED Microraptor** had **2 PAIRS OF WINGS.** The **LARGEST** was about **3 FT 3 IN** (1 m) across.

Deinonychus laid **EGGS** about **3 IN** (7 cm) in diameter, which are thought to have been **BLUE** with **BROWN** spots.

In **1995,** a **14-YEAR-OLD BOY** in Montana found a dromaeosaur that was only **30 IN** (70 cm) long. It was **SO TINY,** it was named **Bambiraptor.**

DROMAEOSAURS WALKED ON 2 LEGS, raising their **SECOND TOE** off the ground. The toe featured a large, curved claw up to **9 IN** (24 cm) long in some species that could hook onto prey.

First discovered in Cretaceous sandstone in Utah in **1991,** the **LARGEST-KNOWN** dromaeosaur is **Utahraptor,** which **MEASURED** up to **23 FT** (7 m) long.

Dramatic
DROMAEOSAURS

Mostly small but always dangerous, dromaeosaurs were raptors that lived from the Middle Jurassic to the Late Cretaceous Period. Closely related to birds, these fast-moving predators had abundant feathers and sharp toe claws. Their fossilized remains have been found on almost every continent.

The bite of **Dromaeosaurus** was **3 TIMES MORE POWERFUL** than that of **Velociraptor**.

Velociraptor
may have reached speeds of
25MPH
(40kph), using its long,
FLEXIBLE TAIL AS A RUDDER
to quickly change direction.

UTAHRAPTOR
WEIGHED up to
770LB
(350kg), about the **SAME** as a
brown bear.

Chomping
CROCODILIANS

Crocodilelike reptiles, with bony plates called osteoderms beneath their scaly skin, have been around since the Late Triassic. They began to evolve into their current form during the Cretaceous but were much more diverse in size, skull shape, diet, and habitat than modern-day crocodiles.

The caiman ancestor **Mourasuchus** lived **8 MILLION YEARS AGO.** It had about **190 SMALL TEETH** and may have collected **CRUSTACEANS** and **FISH** in a jaw pouch like a **PELICAN.**

When the **50-MILLION-YEAR-OLD SERRATED TEETH** of **SEBECUS** were **FIRST DISCOVERED IN 1906** in Argentina, they were thought to be from a **TYRANNOSAURID** that survived the dinosaurs' mass extinction.

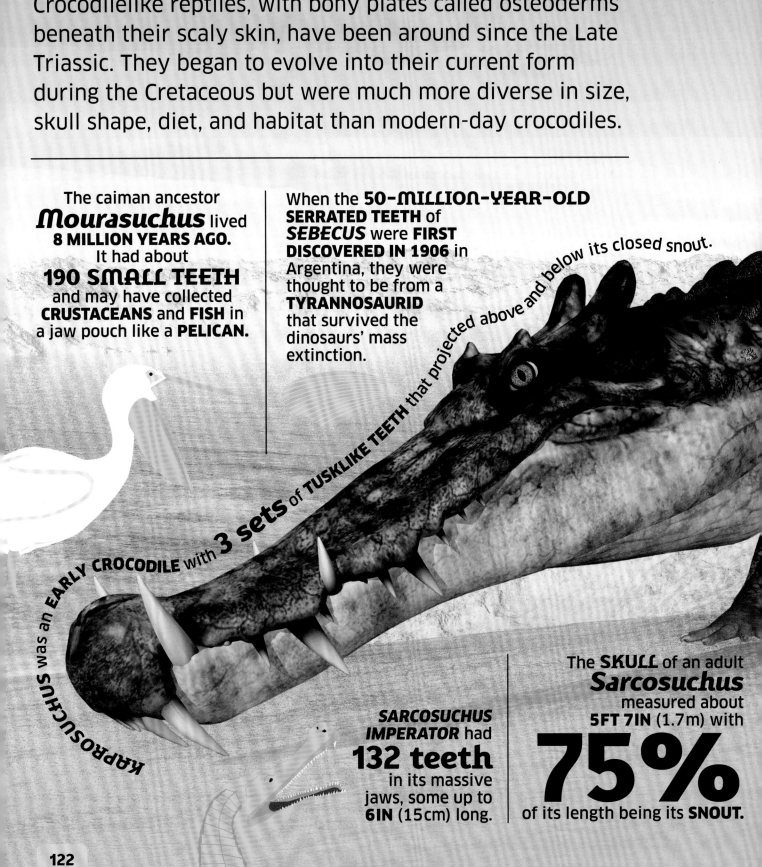

KAPROSUCHUS was an **EARLY CROCODILE** with **3 sets** of **TUSKLIKE TEETH** that projected above and below its closed snout.

SARCOSUCHUS IMPERATOR had **132 teeth** in its massive jaws, some up to **6IN** (15cm) long.

The **SKULL** of an adult **Sarcosuchus** measured about **5FT 7IN** (1.7m) with **75%** of its length being its **SNOUT.**

The tiny **PUG-NOSED** crocodile relative **SIMOSUCHUS** was just

2 FT 6 IN

(75cm) in length and probably a **HERBIVORE.**

Protosuchus
("FIRST CROCODILE") dates to the **JURASSIC.** It was

3 FT 3 IN

(1m) long and stood **MORE UPRIGHT** than **MODERN CROCODILES,** which meant it could run faster.

The small **"RAT CROC"** *Araripesuchus* had **2 BUCKTEETH** in its lower jaw for digging up **GRUBS TO EAT.**

The **GIANT ALLIGATOR** ancestor *DEINOSUCHUS* ("terror crocodile") may have crossed paths with **TYRANNOSAURS** but was a **MUCH LARGER PREDATOR** with a skull up to

5 FT

(1.6m) in length.

The prehistoric caiman *PURUSSAURUS BRASILIENSIS* may have had one of the **STRONGEST BITES** of any animal, exerting a pressure of

69,000 NEWTONS,
3.5 times
that of a **GREAT WHITE SHARK.**

Birds are **crocs'** **CLOSEST LIVING RELATIVES,** but their **LAST ANCESTOR IN COMMON** lived around

250 MILLION YEARS AGO.

NIGER'S CRETACEOUS *Laganosuchus* is called the **"PANCAKE CROC"** for its

20 FT- (6m-) long, **FLAT BODY** and **ULTRA-THIN JAWS,** which it held open for fish to swim into.

TOP 5
BIGGEST CROCS

We don't have any complete skeletons of giant prehistoric crocs, but fossils suggest that some crocodile ancestors dwarfed their relatives of today. From the super croc to the terror croc, these massive predators were so fierce, some of them even hunted dinosaurs!

1

SARCOSUCHUS • Early Cretaceous • **AFRICA AND SOUTH AMERICA** • Length: **30–39FT** (9–12m)

This 4-tonne "super croc" with a distinctive overbite could reach an epic size because it had a long time to grow, living 50–60 years. One partial skeleton unearthed in Niger, West Africa, was estimated to be from a creature 38ft (11.65m) long based on its skull size.

2 *DEINOSUCHUS*
Late Cretaceous • **MEXICO AND US**
Length: **26–39FT** (8–12m)

Known as the "terror crocodile", *Deinosuchus* was an ambush predator with teeth as big as bananas. Its whopping bite marks have been found on the bones of giant turtles and dinosaurs that didn't see them lurking at the water's edge. Fossil vertebrae found in Texas and Montana hint at beasts that may have reached up to 39ft (12m) long.

3 *PURUSSAURUS*
Miocene • **SOUTH AMERICA**
Length: **33–36FT** (10–11m)

Prowling the swamplands of today's Amazon region around 8 million years ago, the caiman relative *Purussaurus* was the undisputed top predator of its time. Equipped with deadly rounded chompers, it could snare prey weighing up to a ton.

4 *GRYPOSUCHUS*
Miocene • **SOUTH AMERICA**
Length: **33FT** (10m)

With its long, thin snout, *Gryposuchus* is thought to be among the biggest members of the gharial family. A *G. croizati* specimen from the Late Miocene found in Venezuela was estimated to be 33⅓ft (10.15m) in length.

5 *AEGISUCHUS*
Mid Cretaceous • **MOROCCO, AFRICA**
Length: **29.5FT** (9m)

More than 90 million years ago, *Aegisuchus* stalked the waters of Africa. Its extremely long, flat skull was covered in heavy skin, inspiring its name, which means "shield croc." Scientists speculate that this distinctive noggin helped the crocs communicate and regulate body temperature.

Armored
ANKYLOSAURS

The tanks of the dinosaur age, ankylosaurs were stocky, four-legged plant-eaters that lived from the Middle Jurassic to the Late Cretaceous. As well as a tough, bony armored back, many had heavy tail clubs that they could swing in defense.

The **CLUB** on the **TAIL** of **ANKYLOSAURUS** could measure up to **19IN** (49cm) wide and **24IN** (60cm) long, the **LENGTH OF 2 LARGE SODA BOTTLES.**

The bone-breaking impact force of **ANKYLOSAURUS'S TAIL CLUB** would have been about **2,000 newtons,** the same as a **SEA LION** landing on you.

The **OLDEST ANKYLOSAUR, SPICOMELLUS AFER,** dates to **167** MILLION YEARS AGO and is the only species to have **SPIKES FUSED** to its **RIB BONES.**

A group of **12** fossilized young **Pinacosaurus grangeri** were found together, all in upright positions, which suggests that **ANKYLOSAURS MOVED IN HERDS.**

The **TAIL CLUB** of **ANKYLOSAURUS** was made of **BLOCKS OF BONE** and weighed about **44LB** (20kg), the same as **3 BOWLING BALLS.**

To keep up its weight, **Ankylosaurus** would have had **TO EAT** about **130LB** (60kg) of **PLANTS A DAY.**

Ankylosaurus

was the last and largest of the **ANKYLOSAURS**. It grew to an estimated

30 FT
(9m) in length and

6 FT
(1.8m) in width.

ANKYLOSAURS were **SLOW WALKERS** at

2 MPH
(3kph). They could only run at about

6 MPH
(10kph).

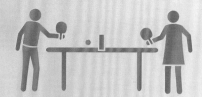

One of the **SMALLEST ANKYLOSAURS** was **Minmi,** a **FRUIT-EATING DINOSAUR** only

10 FT
(3m) long, about the length of a **TABLE-TENNIS TABLE**.

ANKYLOSAURUS could weigh up to

6.6 TONS,
as much as **2 WHITE RHINOS**.

The name **ANKYLOSAUR** means **"FUSED LIZARD,"** referring to the **OSTEODERMS** (bony plates) attached to the dinosaur's **BACK** as **ARMOR**. The **TRIANGULAR PLATES** on *GASTONIA* could be

9 IN
(24cm) long.

ANKYLOSAURUS'S small head was protected by **4 HORNLIKE SPIKES.**

Canada's **BOREALOPELTA MARKMITCHELLI** is one of the

best-preserved dinosaur remains ever
found, complete with fossilized red-brown skin. It took more than

7,000 hours
over **6 years**
to prepare for display.

Carnivorous
CARCHARODONTOSAURS

Including the dinosaurs *Giganotosaurus*, *Carcharodontosaurus*, and *Tyrannotitan*, carcharodontosaurs were some of the largest land predators ever. These two-legged theropods had jaws full of serrated teeth, a feature that inspired their name, which means "shark-toothed lizards."

CARCHARODONTOSAURUS SAHARICUS lived alongside **SPINOSAURUS** in what is now the **SAHARA DESERT** **99 million** **YEARS AGO,** when it was covered in wetlands.

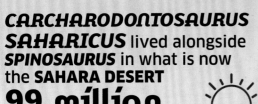

Possibly the **LARGEST CARCHARODONTOSAUR,** *Giganotosaurus* may have reached **41FT** (12.5m) in length, **SIMILAR** to a **TYRANNOSAURUS.**

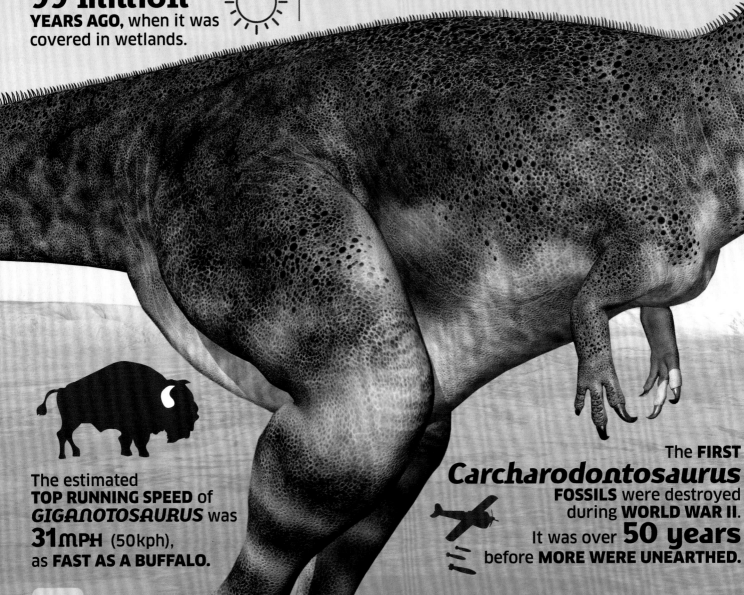

The estimated **TOP RUNNING SPEED** of **GIGANOTOSAURUS** was **31MPH** (50kph), as **FAST AS A BUFFALO.**

The **FIRST** *Carcharodontosaurus* **FOSSILS** were destroyed during **WORLD WAR II.** It was over **50 years** before **MORE WERE UNEARTHED.**

57

Tyrannotítan

TEETH were found among **FOSSIL BONES** of a *Patagotítan,* showing that the predators **SCAVENGED** the gigantic sauropod's **REMAINS.**

MAPUSAURUS was first discovered in **1997** in approximately **90-MILLION-YEAR-OLD** rocks in Argentina.

CARCHARODONTOSAURUS could **lift up to** **935 LB** (424 kg) of **PREY** in its jaws **WITHOUT LOSING ITS BALANCE.**

CARCHARODONTOSAURUS had a relatively **LIGHTWEIGHT SKULL** about **5 FT 3 IN** (1.6 m) long.

Carcharodontosaurus had **62 SERRATED TEETH,** up to **6 IN** (15 cm) long, that sort of resembled those of a **GREAT WHITE SHARK.**

GIGANOTOSAURUS may have weighed up to **9 TONS.**

The remains of **7 Mapusaurus,** ranging in size from **16—36 FT** (5–11 m) long, were found **TOGETHER,** suggesting a **POSSIBLE FAMILY GROUP.**

CARCHARODONTOSAURUS could probably **BITE** with a force of **25,449 NEWTONS,** the equivalent of being crushed by **5 HORSES.**

Crested
LAMBEOSAURS

This group of hadrosaurs (duck-billed dinosaurs) from the Late Cretaceous are known for their hollow, helmetlike head crests. Lambeosaurs, such as *Corythosaurus*, were large plant-eaters that walked on both two and four legs and may have been able to communicate with their herds by blowing through their crests like a trumpet.

A **CORYTHOSAURUS SKULL** dug up in **1920** was **REUNITED** with the rest of its body

92 years later

when the dig site was reexcavated in **2012**.

Corythosaurus
had a **ROUNDED, FLAT CREST** on its head that made its skull

30IN
(75cm) in height.

CORYTHOSAURUS
had a total of

3
HOOFLIKE TOES
on each foot.

Corythosaurus
got its name, meaning **"CORINTHIAN HELMET LIZARD,"** because its crest **RESEMBLED HELMETS** worn by **CORINTHIAN SOLDIERS** **2,500 YEARS AGO.**

CORYTHOSAURUS used its **BEAKLIKE JAW** to **SNIP PLANTS** before **GRINDING** them with

100s
of **CHEEK TEETH** in a **"DENTAL BATTERY."**

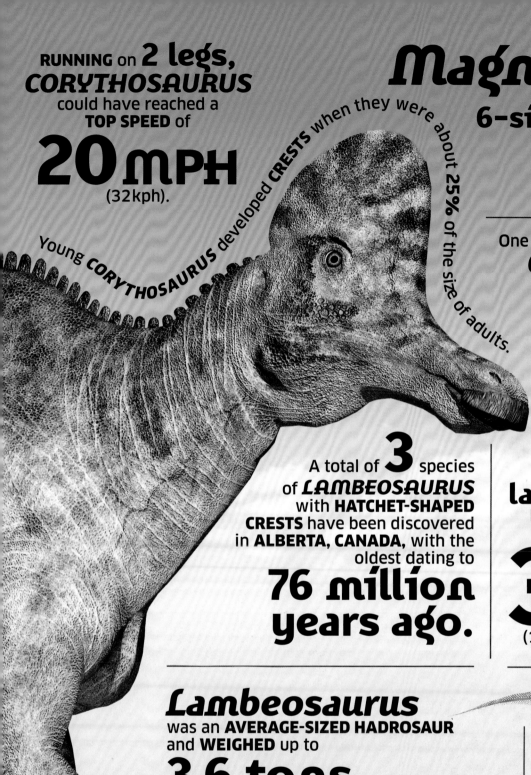

RUNNING on **2 legs,** **CORYTHOSAURUS** could have reached a **TOP SPEED** of

20 MPH
(32kph).

Young **CORYTHOSAURUS** developed **CRESTS** when they were about **25%** of the size of adults.

Magnapaulia
was covered with **6-sided scales,** up to

2/5 IN
(1cm) in width.

One of the best **SPECIMENS** of *Corythosaurus* was found in

1912
and included impressions of **WARTY SKIN** and **TAIL TENDONS.**

A total of **3** species of *LAMBEOSAURUS* with **HATCHET-SHAPED CRESTS** have been discovered in **ALBERTA, CANADA,** with the oldest dating to

76 million years ago.

Possibly the **LONGEST-KNOWN** *lambeosaurine,* **MEXICO'S** *MAGNAPAULIA* grew to more than

39 FT
(12m) from **HEAD TO TAIL.**

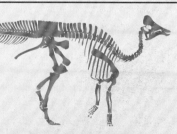

Lambeosaurus
was an **AVERAGE-SIZED HADROSAUR** and **WEIGHED** up to

3.6 tons.

There are **2 early specimens** of **CORYTHOSAURUS** on the bottom of the **ATLANTIC OCEAN,** after **SINKING IN A SHIP** in **1916.**

Unearthed in **1999,** *OLOROTITAN,* a

26 FT-
(8ft-) long hadrosaur with a fanlike crest, is the **MOST-COMPLETE DINOSAUR SKELETON** ever found in **RUSSIA.**

Remarkable
OVIRAPTOROSAURS

These mostly toothless, feathered dinosaurs had long necks and parrotlike beaks. Oviraptorosaurs lived for about 60 million years during the Cretaceous Period. Fossils reveal that they made nests and incubated their eggs.

The **LARGEST-KNOWN** oviraptorosaur was *Gigantoraptor erlianensis,* which grew up to **11 FT 6 IN** (3.5m) high at the hip and **26 FT** (8m) in **TOTAL LENGTH,** as long as a **SCHOOL BUS.**

OVIRAPTOR was named **"EGG THIEF" IN THE 1920s** as its bones were found near eggs. **70 YEARS** later, fossilized embryos proved the eggs to be **OVIRAPTOR'S!**

Early **OVIRAPTOROSAUR** *Caudipteryx* had a **TAIL FAN** of **BANDED FEATHERS** up to **5 IN** (13cm) long.

MACROELONGATOOLITHUS is a name given to a type of **FOSSIL OVIRAPTOROSAUR EGG.** The **GIANT OVAL EGGS** are **3 times** LONGER than they are **WIDE** and measure up to **24IN** (61cm) tall.

A study of **1 GIGANTORAPTOR** showed it grew by **300 LB** (140kg) per year.

Like many **OVIRAPTOROSAURS**, *Anzu wyliei* had a **HEAD CREST** made of **BONE AND KERATIN**. This gave its skull a height up to **12½IN** (32cm), a little taller than this book.

One of the smallest **OVIRAPTORS** was **Caudipteryx**. At just **3FT** (89cm) long, this birdlike dinosaur was the size of a **TURKEY**.

Gigantoraptor erlianensis may have weighed **1.5 TONS**, **280 times** the weight of the **SMALLEST OVIRAPTOROSAUR Caudipteryx**.

OVIRAPTOR grew to about **6FT 6IN** (2m), the same as the average height of an **NBA BASKETBALL PLAYER** but **NOT AS HEAVY** at **88LB** (40kg).

One of the **EARLIEST-KNOWN** oviraptorosaurs, *Incisivosaurus* lived in China around **126 MILLION YEARS AGO**.

CAUDIPTERYX was **TINY** but **FAST**, with a **TOP RUNNING SPEED** of **17MPH** (29kph).

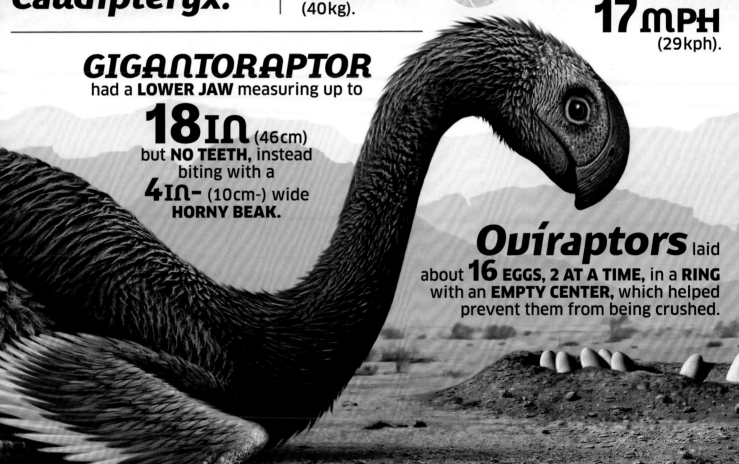

GIGANTORAPTOR had a **LOWER JAW** measuring up to **18IN** (46cm) but **NO TEETH**, instead biting with a **4IN-** (10cm-) wide **HORNY BEAK**.

Oviraptors laid about **16 EGGS, 2 AT A TIME**, in a **RING** with an **EMPTY CENTER**, which helped prevent them from being crushed.

A **10 FT 6 IN-** (3.2m-) **TALL PENTACERATOPS SKULL** on display in Oklahoma is the **LARGEST DINOSAUR SKULL** ever found.

Because of its **SOLID BONE STRUCTURE**, *Triceratops's* skull fossilizes very well. More than **50 SKULL FOSSILS** have been unearthed.

No other ceratopsian was **HEAVIER** than *Triceratops horridus*, which could reach **10 TONS**, around the **WEIGHT** of **8 small cars.**

AGUJACERATOPS was found in **1938** in rocks dating to **77 MILLION** years ago.

The "bison lizard" *Einiosaurus* lived **74 MILLION YEARS** ago. It had **2 SPIKES** on its **FRILL** and **1 large, distinctive nose horn** that **CURVED FORWARD** over its beak.

KOSMOCERATOPS RICHARDSONI had **15 horns** on its **FACE** and **FRILL—NO OTHER ANIMAL** has **HAD MORE.**

The **FIRST EVER** *Zuniceratops* fossil was found in **NEW MEXICO,** by an **8-YEAR-OLD** boy.

Horned
CERATOPSIANS

Ceratopsians were amazing-looking dinosaurs that thrived in the Cretaceous Period. Most of them had huge, sharp horns, long neck frills, and parrotlike beaks for grasping plants. Smaller, lighter ceratopsians could walk on two legs, but later, heavier ceratopsians such as *Triceratops* used all four limbs to support their hefty weight.

NOT ALL ceratopsians were **MASSIVE.** The **CAT-SIZED** *Aquilops americanus* only **WEIGHED 3LB 4OZ** (1.5kg), about the same as **6** cans of soup.

TRICERATOPS, TOROSAURUS, and **COAHUILACERATOPS** had horns up to **4FT** (1.2m) in length, the **LONGEST OF ANY DINOSAUR.**

PROTOCERATOPS kept its eggs warm for at least **83 days.**

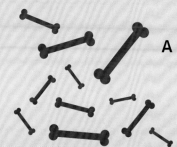

A **FOSSIL BED** of **1000s** of *Centrosaurus* bones was found in **ALBERTA, CANADA,** which may have come from a **HERD THAT DROWNED.**

TRICERATOPS was probably the **LONGEST OF THE CERATOPSIANS** at **30FT** (9m), the **SAME LENGTH** as a **VOLLEYBALL NET.**

ARCHAEOCERATOPS'S name means **"ANCIENT HORNED FACE,"** but although it is a **CERATOPSIAN,** it had **zero horns.**

BIG JOHN

This enormous plant-eater from the Late Cretaceous was unearthed in the famous Hell Creek Formation in South Dakota. Nicknamed after the owner of the ranch where it was found by a professional fossil hunter, "Big John" is the largest *Triceratops* ever discovered.

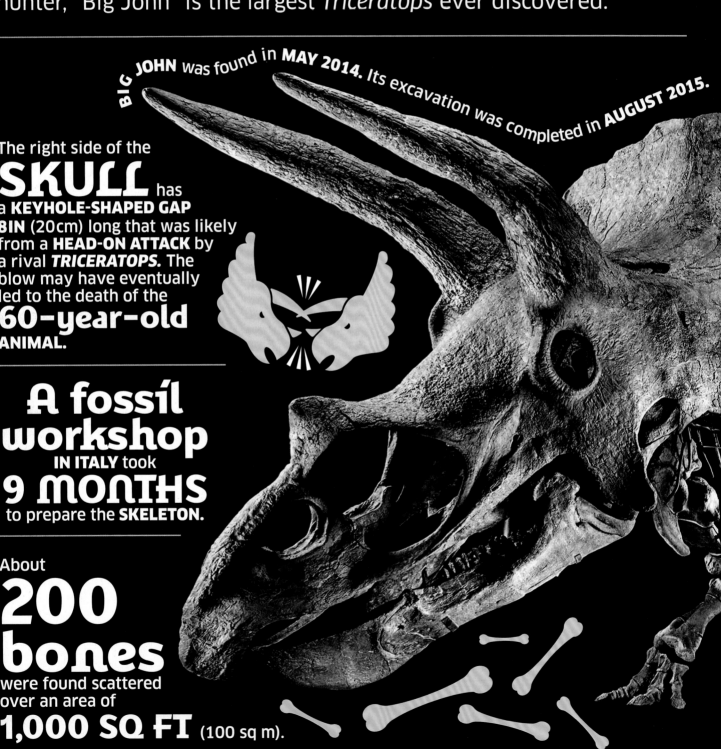

BIG JOHN was found in MAY 2014. Its excavation was completed in AUGUST 2015.

The right side of the
SKULL has
a **KEYHOLE-SHAPED GAP**
8IN (20cm) long that was likely
from a **HEAD-ON ATTACK** by
a rival *TRICERATOPS.* The
blow may have eventually
led to the death of the
60-year-old
ANIMAL.

A fossil workshop
IN ITALY took
9 MONTHS
to prepare the **SKELETON.**

About
200 bones
were found scattered
over an area of
1,000 SQ FT (100 sq m).

More than **100 *TRICERATOPS*** specimens have been unearthed in the **HELL CREEK FORMATION,** making them the most **COMMON DINOSAUR REMAINS** found there.

Big John's skeleton is **5–10% larger** than **ANY OTHER** known ***TRICERATOPS*** specimens.

A **2023** children's museum exhibit made **BIG JOHN** the **FIRST FULL DINOSAUR SKELETON** ever displayed in **TAMPA, FLORIDA.**

Big John is a fossil of the species ***Triceratops horridus,*** which was discovered in Wyoming in **1888** and dates to around **66 million years ago,** the tail end of the **AGE OF DINOSAURS.**

The **SKULL** is **8FT 7IN** (2.62m) **LONG**—more than **1/4** of its **OVERALL BODY LENGTH.**

The **SKELETON** is **60% COMPLETE** and the **SKULL** is **75% COMPLETE.**

Big John was sold at auction in **2021** for **$7.7 MILLION,** making it the **SECOND-MOST EXPENSIVE** dinosaur skeleton purchase of **ALL TIME.**

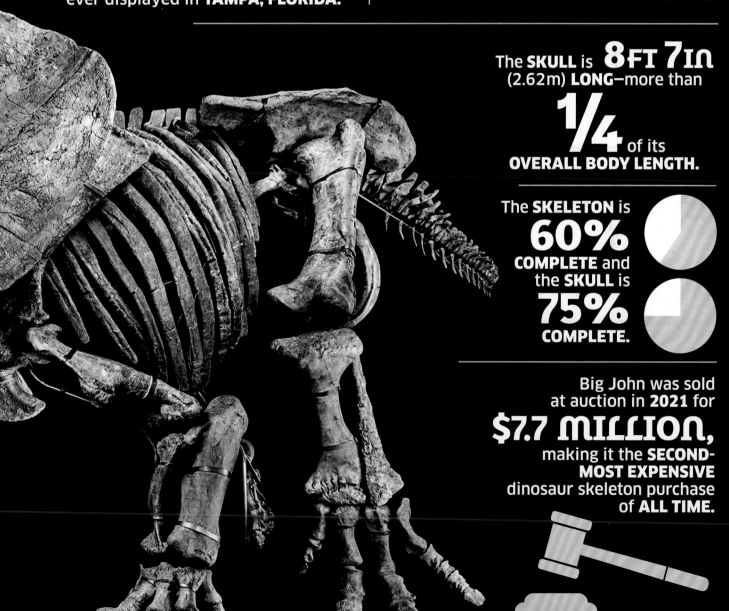

Tremendous
TITANOSAURS

Massive sauropods, the titanosaurs were the largest creatures to ever walk on land. Browsing the tallest treetops during the Cretaceous Period, these plant-eaters were the biggest of the biggest.

DREADNOUGHTUS SCHRANI, from **ARGENTINA**, measured about **85 FT** (26m) long—**LONGER** than the average **REC CENTER SWIMMING POOL.**

Fossils of **AUSTROPOSEIDON MAGNIFICUS** spent **63 YEARS IN STORAGE** before they were **STUDIED** and **DISCOVERED** to belong to a **NEW SPECIES** of titanosaur.

The **FEMUR** (thigh bone) of **PATAGOTITAN MAYORUM** measured **8 FT** (2.4m) in length, **TALLER** than an **ADULT HUMAN.**

Possibly the **LARGEST TITANOSAUR, ARGENTINASAURUS** may have weighed **77 tons,** the same as **10 AFRICAN ELEPHANTS.**

Remains of **TITANOSAURS** have been found on all **7 continents**, including **ANTARCTICA.**

FOSSILIZED REMAINS of titanosaurs are very rare. **PUERTASAURUS** is known from just **4 VERTEBRAE** found in **ARGENTINA** in **2001.**

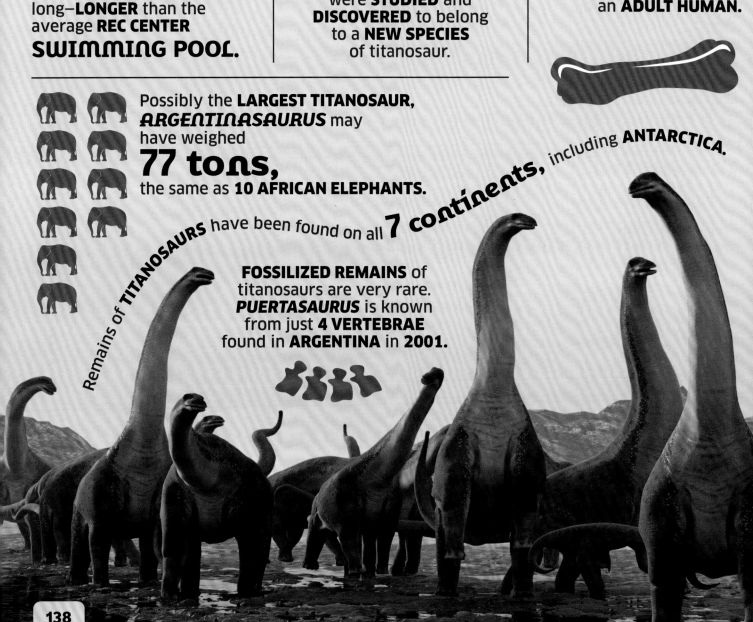

HYPSELOSAURUS PRISCUS eggs are estimated to have been **12 IN** (30cm) in **DIAMETER**, about the size of a **BEACH BALL**.

A titanosaur egg

from **INDIA** remained **UNNOTICED** for

175 YEARS.

It had been **MISIDENTIFIED** and stored in London's Natural History Museum's **MINERAL COLLECTION**.

PALEONTOLOGISTS in **INDIA** discovered

92 titanosaur nests

containing a total of

256

ROUND EGGS.

PATAGOTIAN MAYORUM ate about

284 LB (129 kg)

of **PLANTS EVERY DAY**, the equivalent of

516 HEADS OF LETTUCE.

NOT ALL titanosaurs were **GIANTS**. **MAGYAROSAURUS DACUS** was just **16—20 FT** (5–6m) **LONG** and **WEIGHED** about

2,200 LB (1,000 kg),

the **SAME** as a **LARGE BEAR**.

Evidence of **PARASITIC BLOOD WORMS** just **0.008—0.01 IN** (0.2–0.3mm) **LONG** have been found in the **FOSSILIZED BONES** of some **GIANT TITANOSAURS**.

Ostrichlike
ORNITHOMIMIDS

The dinosaur family name Ornithomimidae means "bird mimics." These feathered theropods from the Late Cretaceous were similar in size and shape to modern-day ostriches. They were fast on their two long legs and mostly plant-eating, with large eyes set in a small skull and a toothless beak.

ORNITHOMIMIDS are named for **BIRDS** they **RESEMBLED,** but they were often much larger. **"GOOSE MIMIC"** *Anserimimus* was **11.5FT** (3.5m) long, **5 TIMES** the size of an **AVERAGE GOOSE.**

PRIMITIVE FEATHERS found on an **ORNITHOMIMUS FOSSIL** measured up to **2IN** (5cm) long and sprouted over its **UPPER BODY, NECK,** and **LIMBS.**

ORNITHOMIMIDS were among the **FASTEST DINOSAURS,** capable of **SPEEDS** up to **37MPH** (60kph), about the **SAME** as a **hyena.**

FOSSILIZED TRACKS and **COLLECTED BONES** suggest *ornithomimids* traveled in **SMALL HERDS** of up to **14 INDIVIDUALS.**

An *Ornithomimus* **SKELETON** found in **ALBERTA, CANADA,** in 2008 was the **first** **DINOSAUR WITH FEATHERS** to be discovered in **THE AMERICAS.**

Ornithomimus had **3 DIGITS** ON EACH **HAND** with 2 fingers and 1 thumb of equal length. It could have used its **CLAWED HANDS** to gather leaves.

Gallimimus

had a brain the size of a **GOLF BALL**, about

1¾IN
(4.3cm) in **DIAMETER**.

The later species of **ORNITHOMIMID** had **zero teeth.** They used **DUCKLIKE BEAKS** made of **KERATIN** to **BITE PLANTS** and **FILTER SMALL PREY** from water.

GALLIMIMUS was the **LARGEST ORNITHOMIMID**, reaching a length of **20ft** (6m).

GALLIMIMUS may have weighed

1,000LB
(450kg), about the same as a **HORSE**.

ARCHAEORNITHOMIMUS, meaning **"ANCIENT BIRD MIMIC,"** is the **EARLIEST ORNITHOMIMID** at **89 MILLION YEARS OLD.**

The best-preserved **ORNITHOMIMID** is a specimen of

Ornithomimus edmontonicus

found in **ALBERTA, CANADA,** in **1995.** The skeleton is almost

100%
COMPLETE, lacking just a few finger bones.

Gallimimus
skulls had **EYE SOCKETS**

3IN (7.5cm) across
for **LARGE, SIDEWAYS-FACING EYES** perfect for **SPOTTING** approaching **PREDATORS.**

The largest-known pachycephalosaur was **PACHYCEPHALOSAURUS WYOMINGENSIS,** which grew to an estimated **23 FT** (7m) in length.

PACHYCEPHALOSAURUS had **SKULLS** up to **32 IN** (80cm) long. Their **FOSSILIZED SKULLCAPS** have been mistaken for **KNEES.**

A **PACHYCEPHLOSAURUS FOSSIL** found in **1860** was misidentified as an **ARMADILLOLIKE** creature for **120 years.**

It is thought that **PACHYCEPHALOSAURS** did not climb. Smaller species would have only **EATEN PLANTS** up to a height of **3 FT** (1m).

PACHYCEPHALOSAURUS had **5 clawed fingers** on each hand.

Of all the **PACHYCEPHALOSAUR** fossils found, **86%** are just **PARTS** of their **SKULLS.**

Named after the **SCHOOL OF MAGIC** in the **HARRY POTTER** books, the **8 FT-** (2.4m-) long **Dracorex hogwartsia** is thought by some scientists to be a young **PACHYCEPHALOSAURUS.**

The bone dome of an **ADULT PACHYCEPHALOSAURUS** skull was the **THICKEST** of any known dinosaur at **8 IN** (20cm), about **20 TIMES THICKER** than **REGULAR** dinosaur skulls.

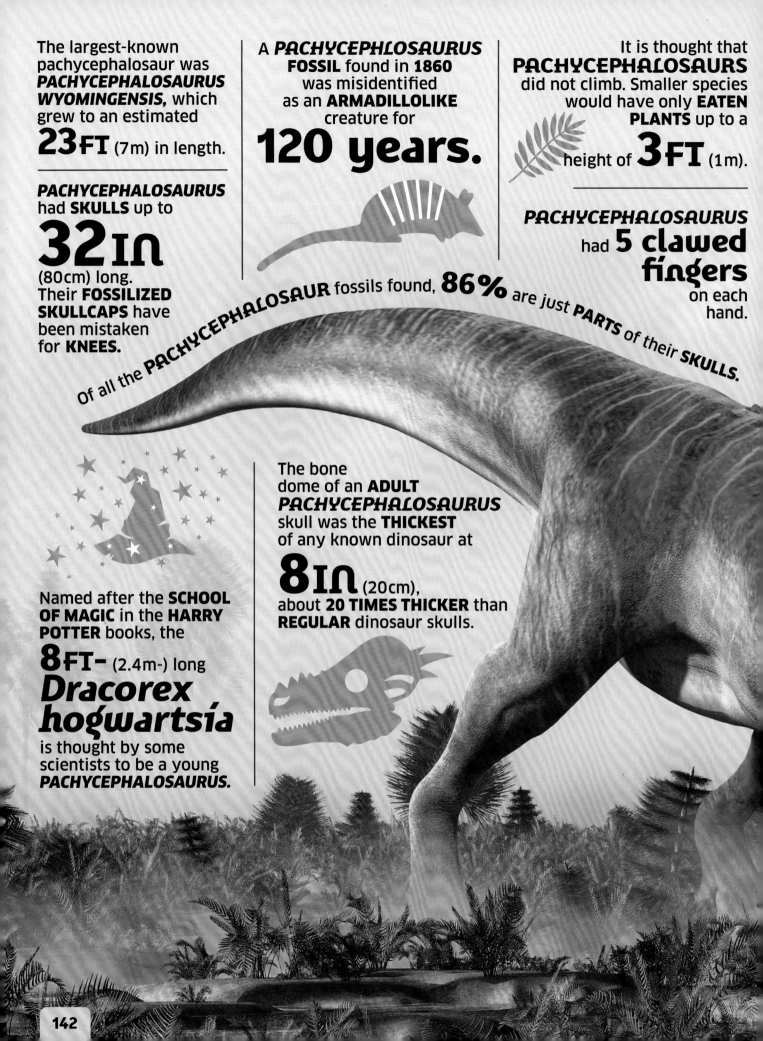

Thick-skulled
PACHYCEPHALOSAURS

These relatively small but famously bone-headed dinosaurs lived during the Late Cretaceous in Asia and North America. Pachycephalosaurs walked on two legs and ate mostly plants. Their tough, sometimes spiky heads were likely used in head-butting competitions between rival males.

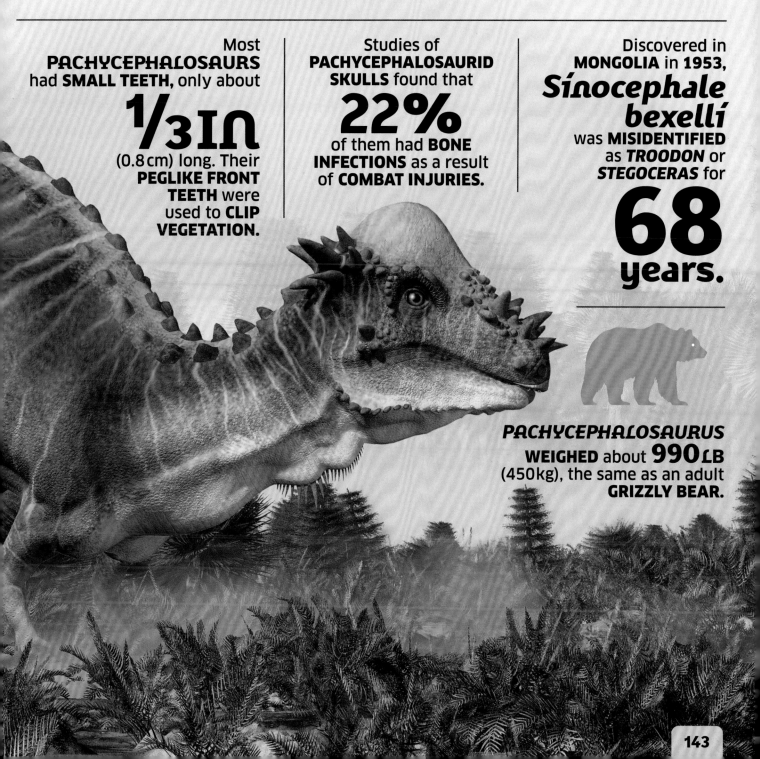

Most **PACHYCEPHALOSAURS** had **SMALL TEETH,** only about

1/3IN

(0.8 cm) long. Their **PEGLIKE FRONT TEETH** were used to **CLIP VEGETATION.**

Studies of **PACHYCEPHALOSAURID SKULLS** found that

22%

of them had **BONE INFECTIONS** as a result of **COMBAT INJURIES.**

Discovered in **MONGOLIA** in **1953,** *Sinocephale bexelli* was **MISIDENTIFIED** as *TROODON* or *STEGOCERAS* for

68 years.

PACHYCEPHALOSAURUS **WEIGHED** about **990 LB** (450 kg), the same as an adult **GRIZZLY BEAR.**

TOP 5
WIDEST
WINGSPANS

Pterosaurs were distant relatives of the dinosaurs and the first vertebrates to take to the sky. In the Cretaceous Period, they included the largest flying animals Earth has ever seen.

1

QUETZALCOATLUS NORTHROPI
Late Cretaceous • **TEXAS**
Wingspan: **36-40FT** (11-12m)

Perhaps the most humongous flying creature ever to have lived, this colossal pterosaur was as tall as a giraffe, hunted like a heron, and soared like a condor. To fly, it had to leap 8ft (2.5m) off the ground.

2 HATZEGOPTERYX THAMBEMA
Late Cretaceous • **TRANSYLVANIA, ROMANIA**
Wingspan: **33-39FT** (10-12m)

Initially identified only from an arm bone and partial skull, this species was named in 2002 based on fossils found outside the town of Hațeg in Romania. Its wingspan is estimated to rival that of *Quetzalcoatlus*, but its skull was even longer!

3 CRYODRAKON BOREAS
Late Cretaceous • **ALBERTA, CANADA**
Wingspan: **AT LEAST 33FT** (10m)

Cryodrakon boreas's large wingspan and heavy build suggest it probably ranged much farther than the couple of sites where partial skeletons have been unearthed. Scientists think the creature, known as the "frozen dragon of the northern winds," could have flown nonstop for thousands of miles.

4 THANATOSDRAKON AMARU
Late Cretaceous • **MENDOZA, ARGENTINA**
Wingspan: **30FT** (9m)

This early giant pterosaur is the largest to have been found in South America, where it once glided over the inland floodplains of what is now Argentina. Its name means "dragon of death," but it probably hunted with its feet on the ground, much like the modern-day Marabou stork.

5 ARAMBOURGIANIA PHILADELPHIAE
Late Cretaceous • **JORDAN AND US**
Wingspan: **26-30FT** (8-9m)

Though the wingspan of this species was slightly smaller than that of other titanic pterosaurs, it had an absurdly long neck—nearly twice the length of that of *Quetzalcoatlus*! With that flamingolike neck, it stood taller than *T. rex*.

Proceratosaurus dates to **170 MILLION YEARS AGO.** It was discovered in **1910** in England from a **PARTIAL SKULL** and is the **OLDEST-KNOWN TYRANNOSAURID.**

T. REX had stapes **(INNER EAR BONES)** up to **240 times LARGER** than ours and could hear very low pitches.

The **FIRST T. REX** was discovered in **1902,** but the **FIRST TINY T. REX ARMS** weren't found for another **86 YEARS.**

SCOTTY, the **LONGEST-LIVED T. REX SPECIMEN** yet found, was **ESTIMATED** to be **30 years old** according to **GROWTH RINGS** in his **BONES.**

Scotty is also the **LARGEST-KNOWN T. REX** at nearly **42 FT** (12.8m) long and **19,555 LB** (8,870kg)—roughly the same weight as **4 PICKUP TRUCKS.**

Tyrannosaurus rex had **60 CONICAL, SERRATED TEETH** that were replaced frequently.

Terrifying
TYRANNOSAURS

These ferocious predators are famous for their tiny arms and massive, bone-crushing bites, yet early tyrannosaurids from the Middle Jurassic were feathered and modest in size. They eventually evolved into the Late-Cretaceous giants we know best, such as *T. rex*.

A dinosaur site in **ALBERTA, CANADA,** where **22** **JUVENILE** and **ADULT** *Albertosaurus* specimens were found, suggests they **MAY HAVE HUNTED IN PACKS.**

At **39 FT** (12m), Mongolia's *TARBOSAURUS* was as long as *T. REX,* but its **TINY 2-CLAWED ARMS** were the **SMALLEST** of any **TYRANNOSAUR** in **RELATION** to its **BODY SIZE.**

At **30 FT** (9m) **LONG,** *Yutyrannus hualí,* discovered by farmers in China, is the **LARGEST ANIMAL** found to date with **DIRECT EVIDENCE OF FEATHERS.**

The **SKULL** of a *DASPLETOSAURUS* found in **2017** suggests that tyrannosaurs had a **MOTION-DETECTING SIXTH SENSE** in their **SENSITIVE SNOUTS** to help **TRACK PREY.**

With the **STRONGEST BITE** of **ANY LAND ANIMAL** in history, *T. rex* could **CLAMP DOWN** with a **FORCE** of up to **6.4 TONS,** the weight of an **elephant.**

A *T. REX SKELETON* sold for **A RECORD** **$31.8 million** at auction in **2020,** making it the **HIGHEST-PRICED FOSSIL SPECIMEN** to date.

Clawsome
THERIZINOSAURS

Therizinosaurs were large, odd-looking herbivores from the Cretaceous. They get their name, meaning "scythe lizards," because the distinctive claws on their forelimbs look like the long, curved blades of scythes. Though good for defense, these were probably most often used to reach high-up plants.

THERIZINOSAURUS'S CLAWS were the **LONGEST OF ANY KNOWN ANIMAL.** They could measure up to

3FT
(91cm).

THERIZINOSAURIDS had **THE LONGEST ARMS** of any **2-legged** theropod dinosaur.

The small **JIANCHANGOSAURUS** had about

110 teeth
hidden behind a **TURTLELIKE BEAK.**

When **THERIZINOSAURUS CLAWS** were found in **1954,** they were thought to belong to a

15FT-
(4.5m-) long **SEA TURTLE.**

Therizinosaurus could reach up to

31FT
(9.6m), the length of **5 BEDS.**

The **AVERAGE LENGTH** of a *Therizinosaurus* leg was

10FT

(3m), taller than an **OSTRICH**.

Found in Alaska,

31 fossilized
THERIZINOSAUR FOOTPRINTS, averaging

8²/5IN

(21.4cm) long, suggest these dinosaurs traveled in **HERDS**.

THERIZINOSAURS are thought to have been **FEATHERED**. Fossils of *Beipiaosaurus* show it was covered in down, with tail feathers

1½−2¾IN

(4-7cm) long.

Therizinosaurs **NESTED IN COLONIES**. In one small area of **MONGOLIA**, fossil hunters found

15 separate clutches

of **THERIZINOSAUR EGGS**−9 of the clutches had **SUCCESSFULLY HATCHED**.

Unlike most **THEROPODS**, *THERIZINOSAURUS* carried its weight on all

4 toes,

rather than keeping one off the ground.

THERIZINOSAUR EGGS were **ROUND** with **ROUGH SHELLS**. The adult that came from an egg **5IN** (13cm) in diameter is estimated to have been **220LB** (100kg).

The small therizinosaurid *ERLIKOSAURUS ANDREWSI* stood at **HUMAN HEIGHT**, but grew to

11FT

(3.4m) in length.

An adult *THERIZINOSAURUS* weighed up to

5.5−6.5 TONS,

as heavy as

10 bull moose.

Menacing
MOSASAURS

Scaly mosasaurs were the dominant marine predators of the Late Cretaceous Period, snapping up fish, sharks, and even plesiosaurs. These whale-sized lizards were similar to modern-day monitors, fast-swimming and monstrous in scale.

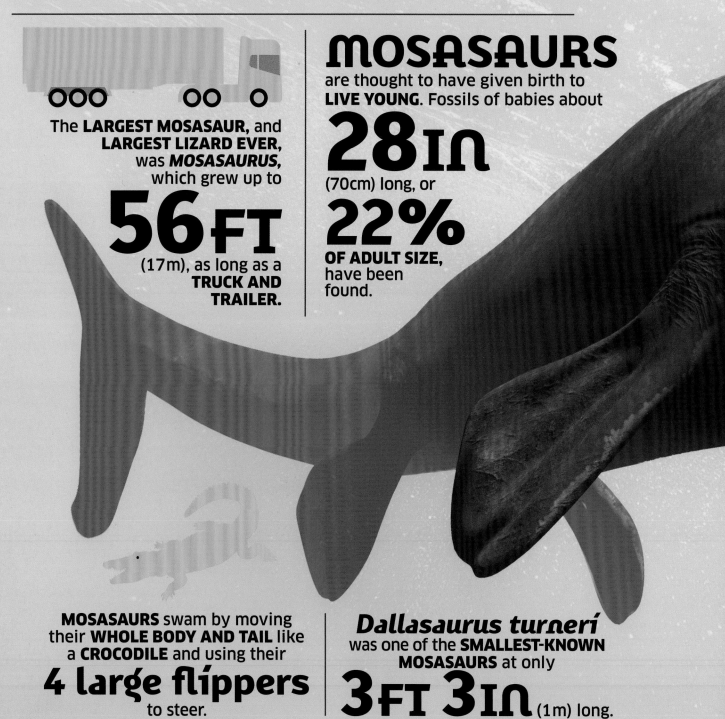

The **LARGEST MOSASAUR,** and **LARGEST LIZARD EVER,** was *MOSASAURUS,* which grew up to

56FT
(17m), as long as a **TRUCK AND TRAILER.**

MOSASAURS
are thought to have given birth to **LIVE YOUNG**. Fossils of babies about

28IN
(70cm) long, or

22%
OF ADULT SIZE, have been found.

MOSASAURS swam by moving their **WHOLE BODY AND TAIL** like a **CROCODILE** and using their

4 large flippers
to steer.

Dallasaurus turneri was one of the **SMALLEST-KNOWN MOSASAURS** at only

3FT 3IN (1m) long.

Tylosaurus had up to **52 conical teeth** in its jaws, which it used to catch **PLESIOSAURS, TURTLES, SEABIRDS, AMMONITES, SHARKS,** and **OTHER FISH.**

The first **MOSASAUR DISCOVERY** was a **JAWBONE** found in the Netherlands in **1764** measuring **3FT 3IN** (1m) in length.

Mosasaurus weighed about **16.5 tons** —as **HEAVY** as **6 HIPPOS.**

MOSASAURUS is thought to have swam near shores at **DEPTHS** of **130—160FT** (40-50m).

FOSSIL IMPRINTS reveal **Tylosaurus** had scaly skin with tiny, **DIAMOND-SHAPED SCALES** measuring about **0.13** by **0.09IN** (3.3 by 2.5mm).

LIKE CROCODILES, MOSASAURS constantly replaced their **TEETH.** It took **Platecarpus 260 days** to **GROW** a **NEW TOOTH.**

The **LARGEST MOSASAUR FOSSIL ON DISPLAY** is a **Tylosaurus pembinensis** named "**BRUCE.**" It measures **43FT** (13m) in length, as long as a **GRAY WHALE.**

One **Mosasaurus missouriensis** fossil includes a **3FT-** (1m-) long **FISH** in its stomach, a meal **50% longer** than the **MOSASAUR'S HEAD.**

The catastrophic
K-Pg EXTINCTION

Around 66 million years ago at the end of the Cretaceous, a huge asteroid hit Earth, sending soot and ash around the world, which blocked out sunlight and caused food chains to collapse. This is when the dinosaurs abruptly died out in an event known as the K-Pg (Cretaceous-Paleogene) extinction.

The **K-PG EXTINCTION** was the

fifth

and **MOST RECENT** major extinction in the past **550 million years.**

All **LAND ANIMALS** weighing more than

55LB

(25kg) died out in the extinction—nothing larger than **A DOG** survived.

Debris from the impact was several times hotter than the *Sun's surface* and set fire to everything within **1,000 MILES** (1,610km).

The **ASTEROID** that **HIT EARTH** was at least

6 MILES

(10km) wide.

The K-Pg Extinction marks the end of the **AGE OF DINOSAURS**, which lasted around **165 million years.**

When the asteroid hit **EARTH**, **27 million tons** of **DEBRIS** were launched into the atmosphere.

Scientists think it took **4 million years** for wildlife in South America to recover.

Small blobs of glass called **microtektites,** formed by the impact of the asteroid, have been found in **HELL CREEK,** **2,000 MILES** (3,200km) away from the impact site.

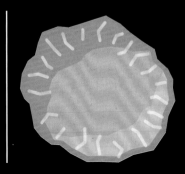

The asteroid hit **EARTH** in what is now Mexico. The impact site, called the **CHICXULUB CRATER,** is about **112 MILES** (180km) wide and was discovered in **1978**.

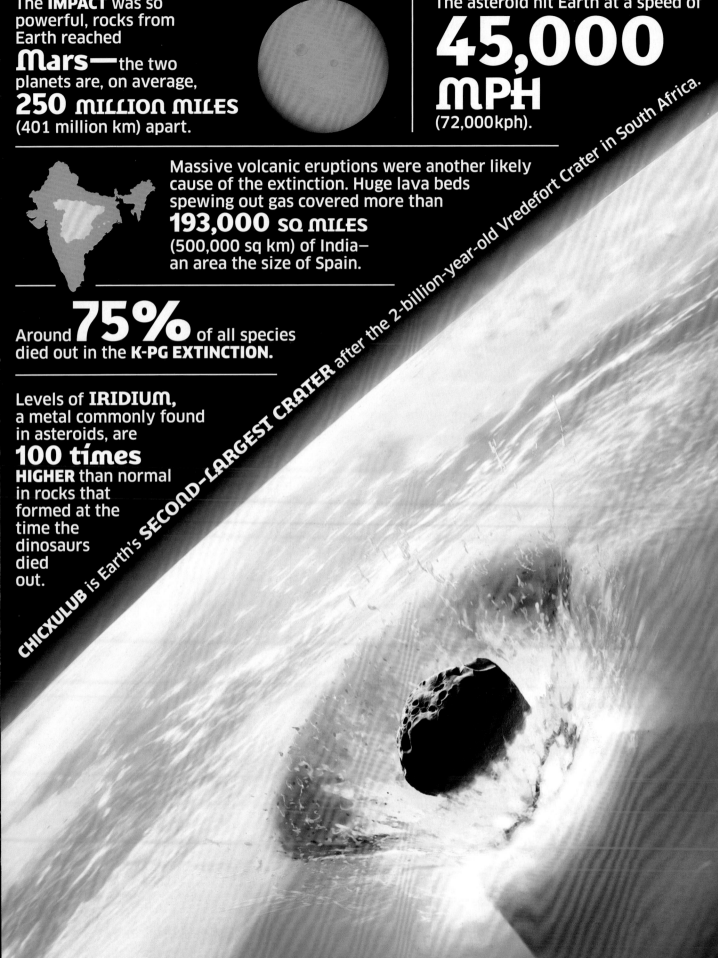

The **IMPACT** was so powerful, rocks from Earth reached

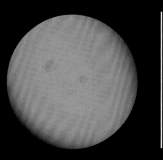

Mars—the two planets are, on average, **250 MILLION MILES** (401 million km) apart.

The asteroid hit Earth at a speed of

45,000 MPH
(72,000kph).

Massive volcanic eruptions were another likely cause of the extinction. Huge lava beds spewing out gas covered more than **193,000 SQ MILES** (500,000 sq km) of India— an area the size of Spain.

Around **75%** of all species died out in the **K-PG EXTINCTION.**

Levels of **IRIDIUM,** a metal commonly found in asteroids, are **100 times HIGHER** than normal in rocks that formed at the time the dinosaurs died out.

CHICXULUB is Earth's **SECOND-LARGEST CRATER** after the 2-billion-year-old Vredefort Crater in South Africa.

AFTER THE DINOSAURS

The **RIVERSLEIGH RAINFOREST KOALA** was **10 TIMES SMALLER** than **TODAY'S LARGEST KOALA.**

The **LARGEST MARSUPIAL** known to exist was **DIPROTODON OPTATUM,** a giant **RELATIVE** of the **WOMBAT** measuring over **12 FT** (3.7m) in length.

The **PREHISTORIC KANGAROO** **Procoptodon** had just **1 TOE** on each **FOOT,** unlike the **4** on **LIVING KANGAROOS.**

Dating to around **25 MILLION YEARS AGO, Chunia** were **EARLY POSSUMS** that are **KNOWN ONLY** from **FOSSILIZED SKULLS.**

The **"MARSUPIAL LION"** **Thylacoleo** had **2 FRONT STABBING TEETH** up to **1.2IN** (3cm) **LONG** in its upper and lower jaws, plus a **DEADLY THUMB CLAW.**

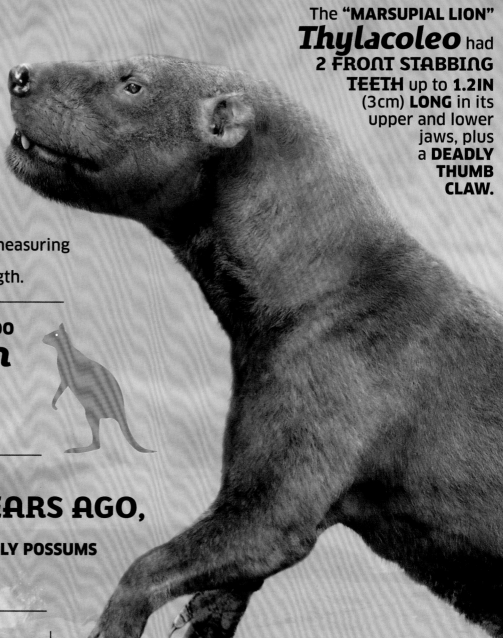

Diprotodon weighed an estimated average of **6,170LB** (2,800kg), **80 times heavier** than a **MODERN-DAY WOMBAT.**

The **EARLIEST-KNOWN MARSUPIAL** is thought to be **DELTATHERIDIUM,** a **RAT-SIZED** creature found in **MONGOLIA** and dating to **80 million years ago.**

Plant-eating **Diprotodon** may have delivered a **BITE FORCE** of **11,134** **NEWTONS,** a little less than that of an **alligator.**

Surprising
MARSUPIALS

This group of mammals gives birth to immature young that usually continue to develop in a pouch. Prehistoric marsupials probably appeared during the Late Cretaceous and spread from the Americas to Antarctica, then to Australia where they evolved into today's kangaroos, possums, wombats, and koalas.

The **LARGEST AUSTRALIAN MARSUPIALS** became **EXTINCT** about **40,000 years ago,** possibly due to **DROUGHT** and **HUNTING BY HUMANS.**

The **6FT 6IN–** (2m–) long, predatory *Callistoe* roamed Argentina around 50 MILLION YEARS AGO.

Like many of today's **4-LEGGED MARSUPIALS,** *Callistoe vincei* had a **BACKWARD-FACING POUCH.**

Australia's largest-ever **CARNIVOROUS MAMMAL** was *Thylacoleo.* It weighed **287LB** (130kg) on average, about the same as a **LIONESS.**

Studies suggest that *Diprotodon* **MIGRATED** about **120 MILES** (200 km) across Australia every year.

The **LARGEST-EVER KANGAROO** was the flat-faced *Procoptodon goliah,* which stood at a height of at least **6FT 6IN** (2m).

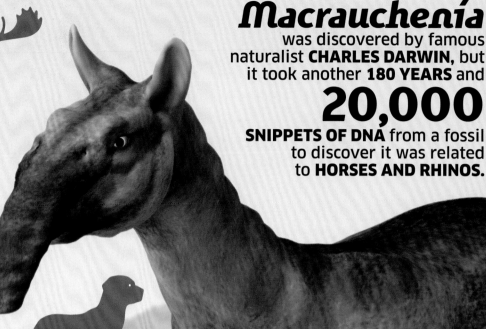

The male
Megaloceros
had **HUGE ANTLERS**
that could be
12 FT
(3.6m) across. That's
TWICE THE SPAN
of those of the
BULL MOOSE, the
largest deer living now.

All hoofed mammals
evolved from ancestors
with **5 TOES** on
each foot, but some toes
WITHERED AWAY, leaving
3, 2, OR JUST 1 TOE.

MESOHIPPUS was
the **FIRST** of the
3-toed horses
and was about the
size of a **LABRADOR.**

Macrauchenia
was discovered by famous
naturalist **CHARLES DARWIN,** but
it took another **180 YEARS** and
20,000
SNIPPETS OF DNA from a fossil
to discover it was related
to **HORSES AND RHINOS.**

Preserved **VOCAL CORDS**
were found within
1 *Mesoreodon*
FOSSIL that revealed it
could **MAKE HOOTING
SOUNDS** like a
HOWLER MONKEY.

CHALICOTHERIUM
had such **LONG CLAWS**
on its **2 front limbs**
that it had to
**WALK ON
ITS KNUCKLES.**

The
10 FT-
(3m-) long
MEGACEROPS
was **RELATED TO HORSES AND RHINOS,**
but, with its **Y-SHAPED HORNS** and **BIG
BUILD,** it looked more like the latter.

Aurochs
were hardy,
6FT- (1.8m-) tall
WILD OXEN from the
PLEISTOCENE EPOCH.
Some were **STILL
ALIVE** in **POLAND** just
400 YEARS AGO.

HOOFED MAMMALS

Ungulates (hoofed mammals) first appeared in the Paleocene Epoch about 66 million years ago. The first ungulates were no bigger than cats, but later species grew to be taller than humans. Some looked similar to modern horses and deer, while others were very different.

Macrauchenia appeared in South America 7 MILLION years ago.

Macrauchenia had **2 nostrils** HIGH ON ITS SKULL, indicating it may have had a **SHORT TRUNK.**

Some members of the **BRONTOTHERES FAMILY,** which included *Megacerops,* grew **1,000 times bigger** over **16 MILLION YEARS.**

Like other ruminants, the **12IN-** (30cm-) long, **DEERLIKE LEPTOMERYX** brought up food from its stomach to **chew a second time.**

Pelorovis was one of the **LARGEST WILD CATTLE** ever–its **2 HORNS** were more than **3FT** (1m) long.

The **RHINOLIKE** *Uintatherium* had **6 blunt horns** on its head– and **1 VERY SMALL BRAIN** inside it.

Merychippus, which appeared around **19 MILLION YEARS AGO,** was probably the **first horse** TO FEED ONLY ON GRASS, unlike its **ANCESTORS,** which ate the leaves of other plants.

IN 2018, fishermen from **NORTHERN IRELAND** got a shock when their **CATCH INCLUDED** the massive, **10,500-year-old** skull of a *Megaloceros giganteus.*

A **5-million-year-old** FOSSIL JAW from an **ARCTIC FOX ANCESTOR** was found **13,497 FT** (4,114m) up in the **HIMALAYAS** of **TIBET**, suggesting they evolved there before **MOVING FAR NORTH** during an **ICE AGE**.

Miacis was about the **SIZE** of a **WEASEL** at **12 IN** (30cm) long and lived **HIGH UP IN TREES**, like many other **EARLY CANIFORMS**.

Up to **8 FT** (2.4m) long, **EPICYON** was the **LARGEST-EVER DOG** and weighed about the same as a **MODERN GRIZZLY BEAR**.

Discovered in **1908**, the **400 LB** (180kg) raccoon-ancestor **Chapalmalania** was so large it was **BELIEVED TO BE A BEAR**.

A **2006** analysis of a **15.8-MILLION-YEAR-OLD RHINO BONE** from **PORTUGAL** revealed it had been gnawed on by the bear-dog **Amphicyon giganteus**.

It took experts **DECADES** to **CLASSIFY** the mysterious **9.5 LB** (4.3kg) **EOARCTOS VORAX**, so it was nicknamed **"KITTEN-OTTER-BEAR."**

At **11 FT** (3.4m), the **"GIANT SHORT-FACED BEAR"** **Arctodus** was **LONGER THAN ANY LIVING BEAR** but had a much smaller snout.

HESPEROCYON GREGARIUS was the **first** **SPECIES** of **DOG**.

Cool CANIFORMS

After the giant dinosaurs were wiped out 66 million years ago, larger mammals like the caniforms began to evolve. These include dogs, bears, and foxes, as well as pinnipeds, such as seals and walruses. Most of them walked on all fours, had long snouts, and ate both plants and animals.

Amphicyonid **"BEAR-DOGS"** prowled around **4 CONTINENTS** during the Miocene period.

Caniforms first appeared around **42 MILLION YEARS AGO** and are still around today.

The **EARLIEST BEARS** were **SMALL**, with **SKULLS** less than **3IN** (8cm) long.

Puijila darwini had a skeleton like an **OTTER'S**, but its skull resembled a **SEAL'S**, with **4 INCISOR TEETH** in its bottom jaw instead of the **6** that otters have.

The only known *PUIJILA DARWINI* **FOSSIL** was discovered in **2007**. It was **65% complete** and is **20–24 MILLION YEARS OLD.**

Weighing around **165LB** (75kg), *AENOCYON DIRUS,* known as the **"DIRE WOLF,"** was **HEAVIER** than **MODERN WOLVES** and may have **HUNTED YOUNG MAMMOTHS IN PACKS.**

Gnawing RODENTS

First appearing about 60 million years ago, ancient rodents came in all sizes, and they are identified mainly by their tooth remains. Their teeth are also what make rodents, such as mice, squirrels, and beavers, different from other mammals—they have two pairs of continuously growing front incisors, which they use for gnawing.

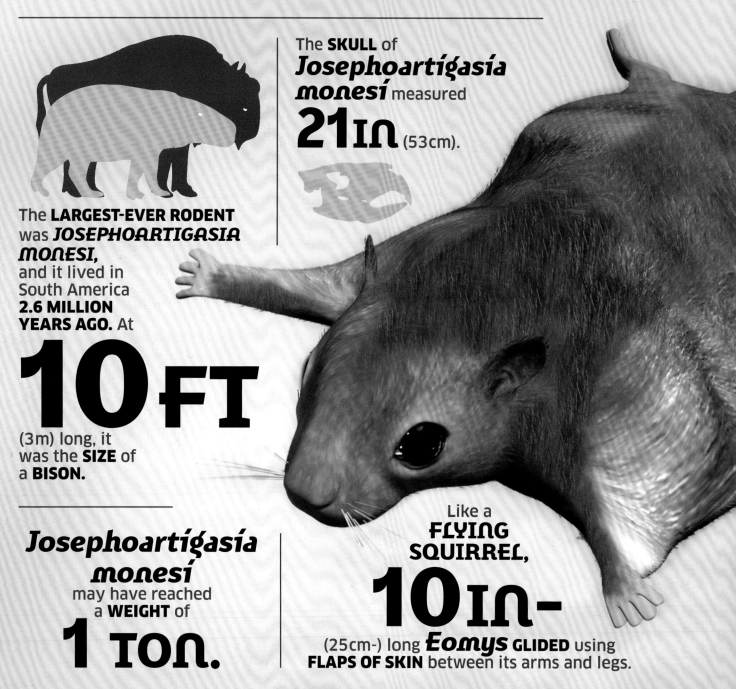

The **SKULL** of *Josephoartigasia monesi* measured **21IN** (53cm).

The **LARGEST-EVER RODENT** was *JOSEPHOARTIGASIA MONESI,* and it lived in South America **2.6 MILLION YEARS AGO.** At **10FT** (3m) long, it was the **SIZE** of a **BISON.**

Josephoartigasia monesi may have reached a **WEIGHT** of **1 TON.**

Like a **FLYING SQUIRREL, 10IN-** (25cm-) long *Eomys* **GLIDED** using **FLAPS OF SKIN** between its arms and legs.

The **OLDEST** fossilized **FLYING SQUIRREL SKELETON** was found in Barcelona, Spain. It is **11.63 MILLION YEARS OLD,** but closely resembles the skeletons of modern **GIANT TREE SQUIRRELS** from **ASIA.**

Eomys quercyi is an early example of a **GLIDING RODENT,** dating to 25 **MILLION YEARS AGO.**

With **2** ¾ **IN** (1.7cm) **SPIKES** above its nose, the **EARLY GOPHER** *CERATOGAULUS* is the **ONLY KNOWN HORNED RODENT.**

In **2019,** an X-ray of a **3-MILLION-YEAR-OLD WOODMOUSE** fossil showed it had **RED FUR,** helping scientists to identify **RED PIGMENTS** in the fossil hair and feathers of other species.

The **CHINCHILLA** relative *Neoepiblema acreensis* weighed a whopping **175LB** (80kg), but its **BRAIN** was a featherlight **1¾ OZ** (47g).

Castoroides was a **BEAVER** the size of a small **BEAR** and lived from **2 million** to **10,000 years ago.**

CASTOROIDES may have weighed up to **275LB** (125kg), **4 times HEAVIER** than a **MODERN BEAVER.**

Castoroides's **GNAWING TOP TEETH** grew to **6IN** (15cm), about as long as a **BALLPOINT PEN.**

The **ANCIENT LAND-DWELLING BEAVER** *Palaeocastor* dug **8FT-** (2.5m-) long, **CORKSCREW-SHAPED BURROWS** with its front teeth.

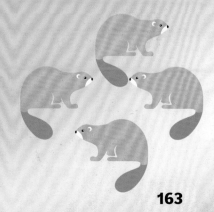

Killer
CATS

Prehistoric cats did not want a lap to curl up in. These fierce predators, which included *Smilodon* (a saber-toothed cat), had muscular bodies and dangerously sharp teeth. Fossils help us determine the beasts' shapes and sizes, but they have yet to reveal whether their coats were plain, striped, or spotted.

SABER-TOOTHED cats and catlike animals **FIRST APPEARED** around **56 MILLION YEARS AGO** and **DIDN'T BECOME EXTINCT** until

11,700 YEARS AGO.

Around **25% LARGER** than **MODERN LIONS**, *Panthera atrox,* or the American lion, was one of the **LARGEST CATS** to **HAVE EVER LIVED.**

A **MODERN LION** can open up its **JAWS** to a **MAXIMUM ANGLE** of

70°.

A *Smilodon's jaws* could open much further to

120°.

The **6 FT-** (2m-) long *Dinofelis* may have **PREYED ON EARLY HUMANS**, as its **BONES** have been **FOUND NEAR SETTLEMENTS.**

In Nebraska,
1 *Nimravus brachyops*'s
TOOTH was found piercing the forelimb bone of another, suggesting that the
2 FIGHTING CATLIKE CRITTERS
may have been **STUCK TOGETHER UNTIL DEATH.**

DNA extracted from the **THIGH BONE** of a
47,000-year-old *HOMOTHERIUM*
contained genes associated with **DAYTIME HUNTING** and **LIVING IN GROUPS** like **LIONS.**

SMILODON'S
2 huge upper canine teeth
grew up to
10IN
(25cm) long. They had a
SAWLIKE rear edge for **SLICING THROUGH PREY** but might have broken if they hit bone.

There were at least
3
SPECIES of
Smilodon.

More than
2,000 SMILODON FATALIS have been recovered from the **LA BREA TAR PITS** in Los Angeles, California.

There were more than 100 types of SABER-TOOTHED CATS.

XENOSMILUS HODSONAE
had **CURVED CANINES**
3½IN
(9cm) long—it is nicknamed the **"COOKIE-CUTTER CAT"** because it gouged out **SEMICIRCULAR CHUNKS OF FLESH** from its **PREY.**

In **2023,**
2 PREVIOUSLY UNKNOWN SPECIES
of saber-toothed cats were discovered in South Africa,
Dinofelis werdelini
and
Lokotunjailurus chimsamyae.

Robust
RHINOCEROSES

Tough-skinned rhinos evolved from tiny, tapirlike hoofed mammals around 50 million years ago. Prehistoric rhinos included the largest land mammal of all time and shaggy two-horned beasts that roamed the planet at the same time as early humans.

The earliest-known **RHINO ANCESTOR** is *HYRACHYUS EXIMIUS,* from **50 million years ago.** This **HORNLESS MAMMAL** was **5FT** (1.5m) long, the size of a **LARGE DOG.**

Wonderfully detailed **cave paintings** of **WOOLLY RHINOS** dating to **30,000 YEARS AGO** show them **BUTTING HORNS** and suggest they had a **BAND OF DARK FUR** around the middle of their bodies.

Paraceratherium linxiaense weighed an estimated **22 TONS,** as much as **A GARBAGE TRUCK.**

Adult male **WOOLLY RHINOS** had a **FRONT HORN** measuring up to **4FT 5IN** (1.35m) long, the height of an **AVERAGE 9-YEAR-OLD CHILD.**

One of the **first** prehistoric rhinos to sport horns was *MENOCERAS,* a pig-sized animal, with **2 SIDE-BY-SIDE HORNS** on its nose.

RHINO HORNS are made of hairlike **KERATIN,** so fossils of them are very rare, but some estimates put an *Elasmotherium* **horn** at **6FT** (1.8m), as tall as an adult human.

ELASMOTHERIUM SIBIRICUM, the "SIBERIAN UNICORN," weighed about **3.8 TONS, 2 times** the weight of a modern rhino.

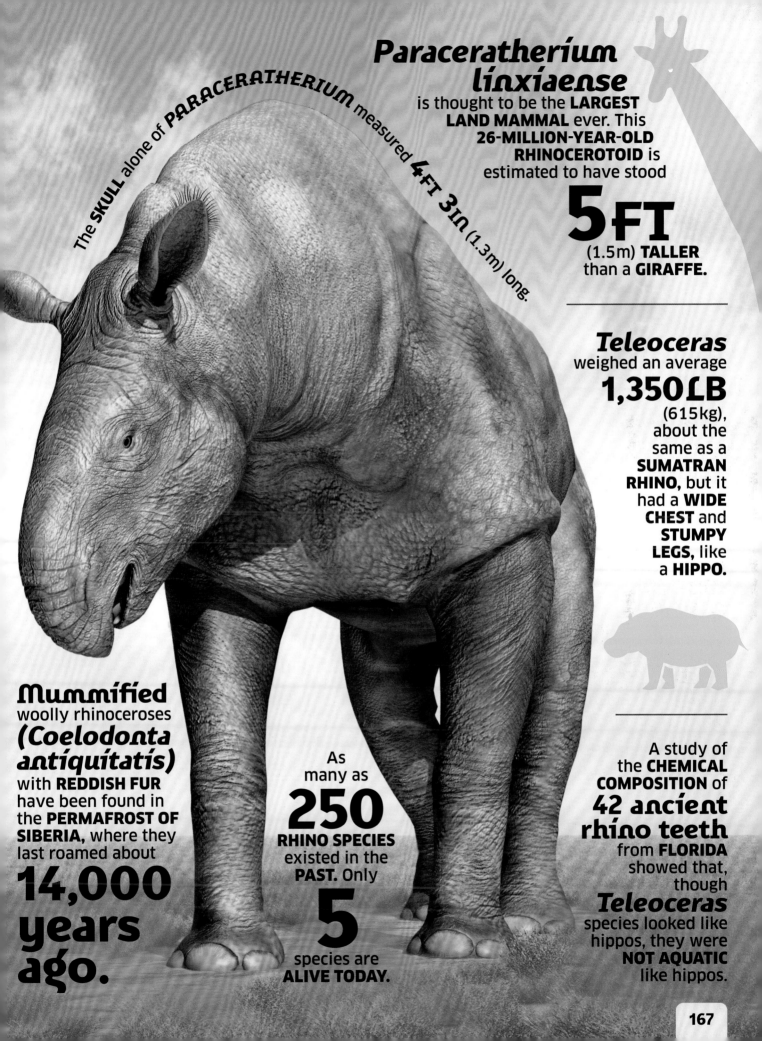

Paraceratherium linxiaense is thought to be the **LARGEST LAND MAMMAL** ever. This **26-MILLION-YEAR-OLD RHINOCEROTOID** is estimated to have stood **5 FT** (1.5m) **TALLER** than a **GIRAFFE**.

The **SKULL** alone of **PARACERATHERIUM** measured **4 FT 3IN** (1.3m) long.

Teleoceras weighed an average **1,350 LB** (615kg), about the same as a **SUMATRAN RHINO,** but it had a **WIDE CHEST** and **STUMPY LEGS,** like a **HIPPO.**

Mummified woolly rhinoceroses **(Coelodonta antiquitatis)** with **REDDISH FUR** have been found in the **PERMAFROST OF SIBERIA,** where they last roamed about **14,000 years ago.**

As many as **250 RHINO SPECIES** existed in the **PAST.** Only **5** species are **ALIVE TODAY.**

A study of the **CHEMICAL COMPOSITION** of **42 ancient rhino teeth** from **FLORIDA** showed that, though *Teleoceras* species looked like hippos, they were **NOT AQUATIC** like hippos.

The **ANCIENT ASH** layer still covers a **250 MILE-** (400km-) long stretch of **NEBRASKA.**

The **ERUPTION RESULTED** in a **layer of volcanic ash** that is between **1FT** (30cm) and **10FT** (3m) **DEEP.**

ASHFALL was **DISCOVERED** in **1971** when paleontologist Mike Voorhies **SPOTTED** the **SKULL OF A BABY RHINO** near his **CAMPSITE AFTER HEAVY RAINS.**

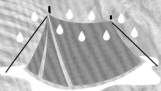

Teleoceras was a **SHORT-LEGGED, BARREL-CHESTED RHINO** that grew up to **13FT** (4m) in length.

Ashfall has been a **STATE PARK** since **1991.** Visitors can enter the **18,000 SQ FT** (1,670 sq m) covered **"BARN"** where specimens are still being **EXCAVATED.**

Hidden beneath a rhino were the bones of *Cynarctus,* a bone-crunching **"RACCOON DOG,"** one of just **2 PREDATORS** found at the site.

The blast was **1,000 times larger** than that of **MOUNT ST. HELENS,** Washington, in 1980, the **MOST DESTRUCTIVE VOLCANIC ERUPTION** in US history.

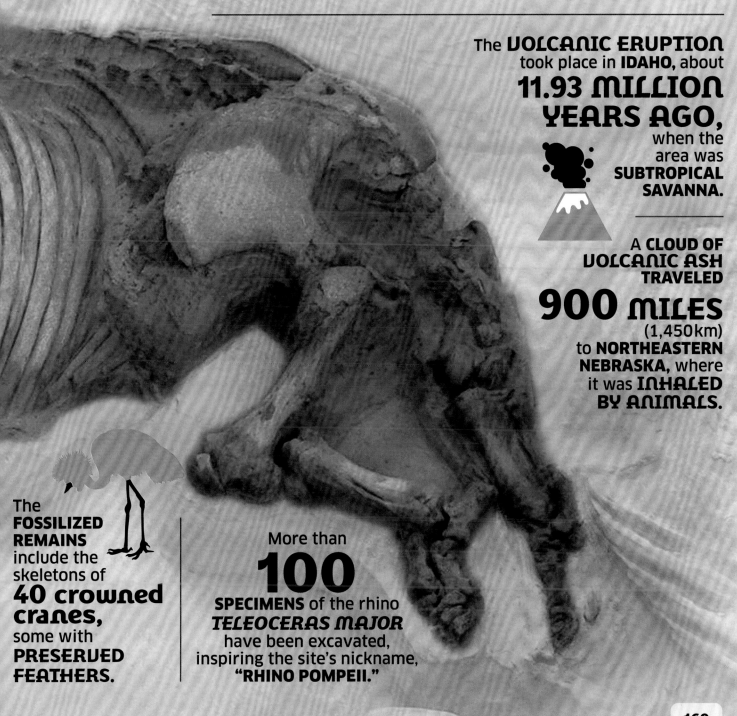

Super finds
ASHFALL BEDS

Tucked away among the cornfields of northeastern Nebraska, the Ashfall Fossil Beds are a remarkable record of a Miocene ecosystem, trapped in time nearly 12 million years ago. After a massive volcanic eruption, savanna animals suffocated in falling ash, while their remains were preserved beneath it.

The **VOLCANIC ERUPTION** took place in **IDAHO,** about **11.93 MILLION YEARS AGO,** when the area was **SUBTROPICAL SAVANNA.**

A **CLOUD OF VOLCANIC ASH TRAVELED 900 MILES** (1,450km) to **NORTHEASTERN NEBRASKA,** where it was **INHALED BY ANIMALS.**

The **FOSSILIZED REMAINS** include the skeletons of **40 crowned cranes,** some with **PRESERVED FEATHERS.**

More than **100 SPECIMENS** of the rhino *TELEOCERAS MAJOR* have been excavated, inspiring the site's nickname, **"RHINO POMPEII."**

Wondrous WHALES

These giant marine mammals evolved from land animals that moved into the water about 50 million years ago. Over time, their limbs adapted into flippers, but they remained air-breathers that fed their young with milk. Some prehistoric whales were apex (top) predators and, like today's orcas, attacked other whales.

At first, **Basilosaurus** was thought to be a **100FT-** (30m-) long **MARINE REPTILE** rather than a considerably shorter whale and was given a name meaning **"KING LIZARD."**

Basilosaurus had **42** **TRIANGULAR TEETH** for **BITING** and **CRUSHING PREY.**

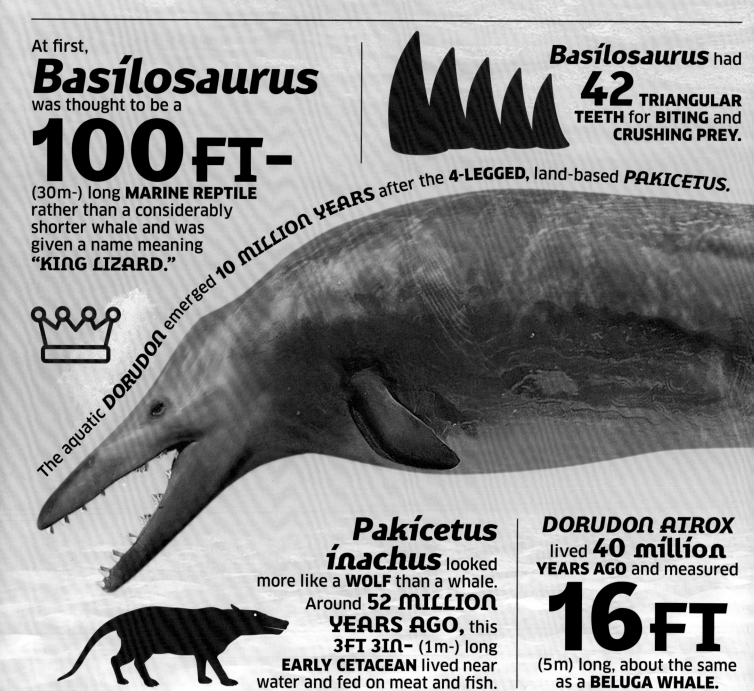

The aquatic **DORUDON** emerged **10 MILLION YEARS** after the **4-LEGGED**, land-based **PAKICETUS.**

Pakicetus inachus looked more like a **WOLF** than a whale. Around **52 MILLION YEARS AGO**, this **3FT 3IN-** (1m-) long **EARLY CETACEAN** lived near water and fed on meat and fish.

DORUDON ATROX lived **40 million YEARS AGO** and measured **16FT** (5m) long, about the same as a **BELUGA WHALE.**

With a name meaning **"WALKING WHALE,"** *Ambulocetus natans* was a

10 FT-

(3m-) long, **4-limbed mammal** the size of a male **SEA LION** that **SWAM** like an **OTTER** and had a **LONG SNOUT.**

Basilosaurus

was a huge marine predator, growing up to

60 FT (18m)

in length, as long as a **SPERM WHALE.**

BASILOSAURUS was

3 TIMES

the size of a **DORUDON.** **FOSSILS** suggest it fed on the **SMALLER WHALE'S CALVES.**

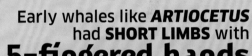

Early whales like **ARTIOCETUS** had **SHORT LIMBS** with

5-fingered hands

and **4-toed feet.** They may have **COME ASHORE** to mate and **GIVE BIRTH** like **SEA LIONS.**

A single **FOSSILIZED** *Basilosaurus* **VERTEBRA** weighs

35 LB (16kg),

about the same as

2

CAR TIRES.

Named after the **EGYPTIAN PHARAOH TUTANKHAMUN,** *TUTCETUS RAYANENSIS* is the smallest-known **BASILOSAUR** at just

8 FT

(2.5m) long.

With its **THICK, DENSE BONES,** the ancient whale

Perucetus colossus

is a possible candidate for the **HEAVIEST CREATURE** to have **LIVED ON EARTH** with a top estimated weight of

375 TONS.

However, many experts think the **BLUE WHALE** probably still holds the title at **297 TONS.**

FOSSIL FOOTPRINTS found in Argentina in **2023** suggest that the **TERROR BIRD** that made them ran on **2 toes,** keeping the **THIRD TOE** free for pinning down its victim.

All **TERROR BIRDS,** also called **PHORUSRHACIDS,** lived in South America, **except for 1, TITANIS,** fossils of which have been found in **NORTH AMERICA.**

The closest living relatives of Madagascar's extinct **elephant birds** are New Zealand's **KIWIS.** They share a **COMMON ANCESTOR** that lived **54 MILLION** years ago.

Titanis was TALLER than an adult human at **6FT 6IN** (2m)–and at **330LB** (150kg), **TWICE AS HEAVY.**

Titanis could run at **40MPH** (65kph)–almost the top speed of a **GREYHOUND.**

When *Phorusrhacos* was discovered in **1887,** it was thought to be an enormous **INSECT-EATING MAMMAL.**

TERROR BIRDS had **2 tiny wings** with **SHARP CLAWS** at the end for attack and defense.

Today only **1 bird,** the **HOATZIN,** has **USABLE CLAWS ON ITS WINGS,** and they only have them as chicks.

Not all **terror birds** would have towered over us– *LLALLAWAVIS SCAGLIAI*– discovered in **2010,** was a not-that-scary **4FT** (1.2m) tall.

Fearsome
FLIGHTLESS BIRDS

Even after top predators like *T. rex* were wiped out, surviving dinosaurs, in the form of "terror birds," still reigned for millions of years. These feathered beasts from the Americas ate smaller animals, so there was plenty on the menu. Other ancient flightless birds were peaceful herbivores but looked just as impressive!

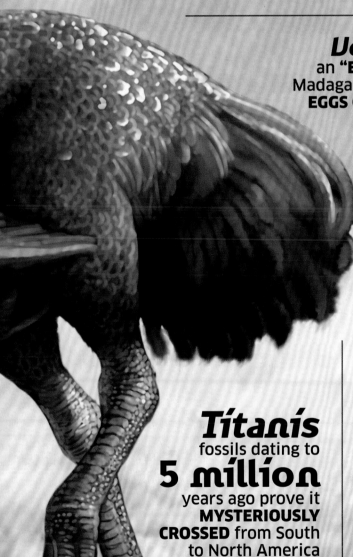

Vorombe titan, an **"ELEPHANT BIRD"** from Madagascar, laid the **LARGEST EGGS OF ANY VERTEBRATE.** With shells more than **12 IN** (30cm) long, they were around **150 TIMES BIGGER** than a chicken egg.

Wingless ***VOROMBE TITAN*** was the **HEAVIEST BIRD SPECIES** that ever existed—at **1,700 LB** (800kg), it weighed about the **SAME AS A BULL.**

The long-necked ***DINORNIS*** was the **TALLEST FLIGHTLESS BIRD** to ever live, reaching **12 FT** (3.6m). That's about **2 times** the height of today's tallest bird, the **OSTRICH.**

Titanis fossils dating to **5 million** years ago prove it **MYSTERIOUSLY CROSSED** from South to North America **1.5 million** years before there was a **LAND BRIDGE** between them.

Dinornis first appeared in **NEW ZEALAND** around **2 MILLION YEARS** ago, and it only died out around **500 YEARS AGO,** hunted **TO EXTINCTION** by humans.

Heavy-shelled
GLYPTODONTS

These armored creatures were giant plant-eating armadillos that appeared 38 million years ago. Glyptodonts lived in South America before spreading to North America after the continents joined. They survived until about 11,000 years ago, when they lived alongside humans.

GLYPTODONTS shared the grasslands of **SOUTH AMERICA** with humans for more than

2,000 years.

The size of a **SMALL CAR,** the hefty

Doedicurus

grew up to **12FT** (3.6m) in length, almost

50 times

LONGER than the average **MODERN ARMADILLO.**

The **ARMORED SHELL** that covered **GLYPTODON'S HEAD** and **BACK** was made up of

1,800
SCUTES (bony scales).

In spite of their bulk, **GLYPTODONS** could **RAISE UP** onto their **2 HIND LEGS** and turn

180 degrees.

Like **MODERN-DAY COWS,** glyptodonts had **8 TEETH IN EACH CHEEK** for chewing plants but **NO CANINES OR INCISORS.**

GLYPTODON ARMOR was

1IN (2.5cm)
THICK in places.

The **LARGEST** of the **GLYPTODON** species probably **WEIGHED** around

4,400LB

(2,000kg).

Glyptodon's SHELL could weigh **1,100LB** (500kg),

20%

of its **TOTAL WEIGHT.**

GLYPTODONTS had unique shell patterns. **GLYPTOTHERIUM** had mostly

6-sided

(HEXAGONAL) SCUTES on its shell.

GLYPTODON'S TAIL had **8–9 rings** made up of **THICK, SPIKY SCALES.**

One **GLYPTOTHERIUM** skull fossil has **2 puncture wounds** from the **BITE** of a **SABER-TOOTHED CAT.**

GLYPTOTHERIUM was discovered by 2 CIVIL ENGINEERS in MEXICO in the 1870s.

Doedicurus had a **SPIKED CLUB** at the end of its **3FT 3IN-** (1m-) long **TAIL** that **WEIGHED** up to

143LB

(65kg).

DOEDICURUS could have swung its lethal **TAIL CLUB** at a **SPEED** of

34MPH

(54kph) to deal blows to **RIVALS** and **PREDATORS.**

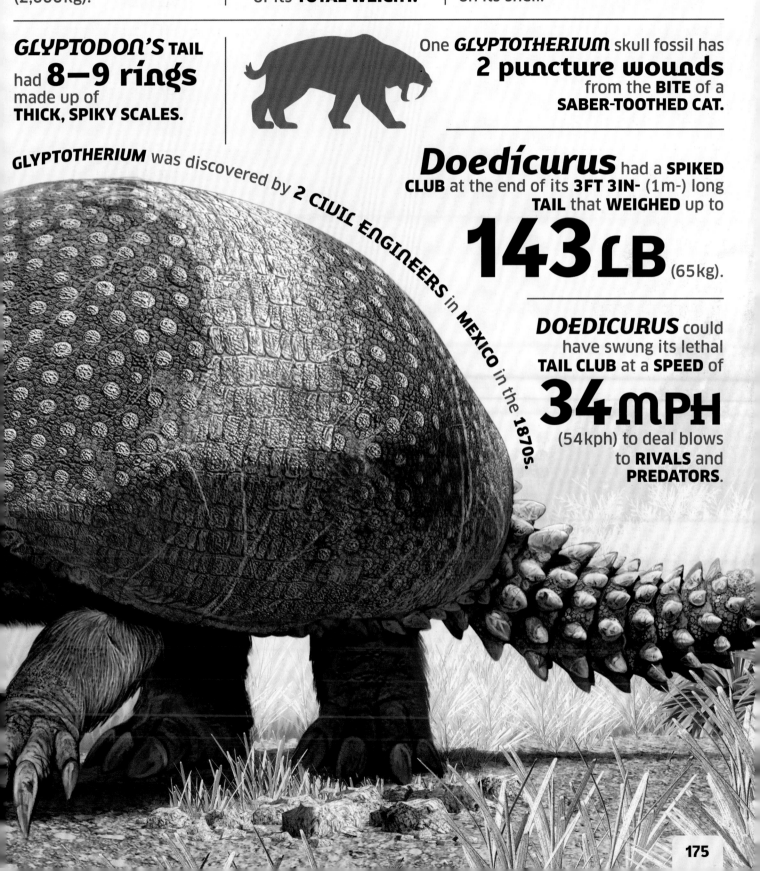

Spry
PRIMATES

The first primates began to appear after the K-Pg Extinction. These early squirrel-like creatures eventually evolved into lemur-type animals and early monkeys, with apes appearing about 25 million years ago. Distinguished by big brains and grasping hands with nails, around 500 species of primates exist today–including humans.

GIGANTOPITHECUS was the **LARGEST APE** that ever lived. At

9FT
(2.7m) **TALL**, it was **TWICE AS BIG** as a **GORILLA**.

The ancient **MOUSE-SIZED** **PURGATORIUS** was only

6IN
(15cm) **LONG**.

First identified from a **JAWBONE** in **1870**, **Notharctus** was assumed to be a **RHINO** but turned out to be a

16IN–
(40cm-) long lemurlike **TREE DWELLER**.

PALAEOPROPITHECUS had **CURVED BONES** with a **60° BEND** in some arm and leg bones.

Purgatorius

could be the **WORLD'S OLDEST PRIMATE,** as fossils suggest it **MAY HAVE BEEN ALIVE** when the **ASTEROID** struck **EARTH** **66 million years ago.**

The **BRAIN** of human ancestor **HOMO ERGASTER** was **52 cubic in** (850 cubic cm). That's **30 CUBIC IN** (500 cubic cm) **LESS** than that of a **MODERN HOMO SAPIENS.**

SAHELANTHROPUS was one of the **first apes** to **WALK UPRIGHT,** around **7 MILLION YEARS AGO.**

WEIGHING up to **660LB** (300kg), the **BIGGEST PRIMATE** *Gigantopithecus* was **FIRST DISCOVERED** in **1935** in a Hong Kong shop, where its molar was being sold as a **"DRAGON TOOTH."**

Homo habilis

("HANDY MAN") appeared as early as **2.8 MILLION YEARS AGO** —and made **STONE TOOLS.**

What looked like **HUMAN FOOTPRINTS** in **TANZANIA** turned out to be made by *AUSTRALOPITHECUS* **3.6 million years ago.**

DARWINIUS,

which lived in **GERMANY** **47 million years ago,** was named to celebrate the **200TH ANNIVERSARY** of naturalist **CHARLES DARWIN'S BIRTH.**

Eosimias

only weighed about **4OZ** (115g)–this **MINI MONKEY** was **SMALLER** than a **HUMAN HAND.**

TOP 5
GIANT SLOTHS

During the last ice age, there was a lot more "megafauna" roaming around—animals weighing more than a ton. Surprisingly, prehistoric sloths were among the very biggest of them, with frames so enormous, their fossil skeletons have often been mistaken for those of dinosaurs!

1 *EREMOTHERIUM* • Pleistocene • **NORTH AND SOUTH AMERICA** • Size: **20FT** (6m) and **6.5 TONS**

Called a "ground sloth" because it stayed on the ground, this gargantuan plant-eater with massive claws first appeared 5 million years ago. Standing 13ft (4m) on its hind legs, *E. laurillardi* was the largest species and at least 800 times bigger than today's tree sloths.

2 *MEGATHERIUM*
Pleistocene • **SOUTH AMERICA**
Size: **20FT** (6m) and **5 TONS**

The South American *Megatherium* ("giant beast") rivalled its close relative *Eremotherium* in size. It lived in a warm climate and may have been almost hairless, like an elephant. The discovery of this giant sloth in Argentina in 1788 sparked one of the first fossil crazes. A few, sparse fossil bone finds show there were other mega species related to *Megatherium*.

3 *LESTODON*
Pliocene to Pleistocene • **SOUTH AMERICA**
Size: **15FT** (4.6m) and **3.9 TONS**

There is only one known species of this tusked ground sloth, *L. armatus*, but its fossils are abundant in the Pleistocene bone beds of South America. Thirteen *Lestodon* of all ages were recently uncovered at one site in Argentina, suggesting they lived in small herds for protection from predators.

4 *GLOSSOTHERIUM*
Pleistocene • **CENTRAL AND SOUTH AMERICA**
Size: **13FT** (4m) and **1.6 TONS**

This grass-eater whose name means "tongue beast" was one of the largest burrowing animals of all time. Two relatives of *Glossotherium*—*Mylodon* of southern South America and *Paramylodon* of North America—were roughly the same size.

5 *MEGALONYX*
Pleistocene • **US**
Size: **10FT** (3m) and **1.4 TONS**

The earliest fossils of this creature, found in a cave in West Virginia, were first described in 1797 by future US president Thomas Jefferson. He thought it was a big cat, giving it a name that means "giant claw." Other fossil finds suggest the furry *Megalonyx* made dens in caves.

Magnificent MAMMOTHS

This extinct group of elephants, *Mammuthus*, roamed much of the Earth during the Pleistocene, an epoch that began 2.6 million years ago. Many were equipped for the chilly Ice Age tundra with shaggy coats and thick, insulating fat. Some epic mammoth remains have been preserved in permafrost.

The huge size of the **woolly mammoth** made it a **TRICKY TARGET** for predators—it **WEIGHED** up to **8.8 TONS.**

A chemical analysis of the growth rings on a **17,000-YEAR-OLD TUSK** revealed that in **28 years,** the **MAMMOTH** it belonged to **WALKED** almost **50,000 MILES** (80,500km)—that's almost **TWICE ROUND THE WORLD.**

Mammoths might have produced **400LB** (180kg) of **POO EVERY DAY.**

PREHISTORIC PEOPLE used **MAMMOTH BONES AND TUSKS** to build **OVAL-SHAPED HUTS.** Around **30 CLUSTERS** of these huts have been found in **EASTERN EUROPE.**

A study of **98 woolly mammoth** specimens found in **SIBERIA** revealed that **70% were male,** suggesting that males probably **LIVED APART** from the **FEMALE-LED HERDS.**

The **PYGMY MAMMOTH** *M. exilis* **EVOLVED IN ISOLATION** on California's Channel Islands. It was **10 times LIGHTER** than its mainland ancestors.

Some **WOOLLY MAMMOTH HAIRS** measured more than **3FT** (1m) long, the **SAME LENGTH** as a **BASEBALL BAT.**

Enormous **COLUMBIAN MAMMOTHS** had **TWISTING TUSKS** up to

16 FT

(4.9m) long, the **SIZE** of a **STANDARD CANOE.**

WOOLLY MAMMOTHS used their

2 spiral tusks

to push down trees, dig in the ground, and fight other mammoths.

The mummy of a

42,000–YEAR-OLD

BABY MAMMOTH nicknamed **"LYUBA"** was found by a reindeer herder near a frozen river in **2007.** She is one of the **BEST-PRESERVED SPECIMENS** of all time.

Both **MALE** and **FEMALE**

mammoths

had **TUSKS,** even when young. These **ADAPTED FRONT TEETH** grew as much as

6 IN (15cm)

in **ONE YEAR.**

The last of the woolly mammoths **DIED OUT** around

4,000

YEARS AGO, so they were **STILL ALIVE** when the **GREAT PYRAMIDS** of **GIZA** were built in **EGYPT,** around **2500 BCE.**

Mammoths spent up to **18 HOURS** each day grazing for as much as **660LB** (300kg) of food.

Many **mammoths** had

2 LAYERS

OF HAIR— a short, yellowish-brown undercoat covered by long, dark brown hair.

Modern-day
DINOSAURS

Do you think that all dinosaurs are extinct? Well, think again! Birds belong to the same group of dinosaurs as *Velociraptor*—they're both two-legged theropods. Toothed birds died out at the end of the Cretaceous along with *T. rex*, but some of their beaked relatives survived, especially those that nested on the ground or could fly.

Birdlike dinosaurs began to evolve around **160 million years ago.**

There are around **11,000 species** of **BIRDS LIVING NOW.** So, though we have only discovered and named around **1,500 extinct species** of **DINOSAURS** thus far, there were no doubt thousands more.

English naturalist **THOMAS HENRY HUXLEY** was the **FIRST PERSON** to suggest dinosaurs and birds were related, in 1869.

Most **MODERN BIRDS** and **THEROPOD DINOSAURS** have **FEET WITH** **3 main toes** and share other features such as **BEAKS, LIGHTWEIGHT BONES,** and **FEATHERS.**

Researchers compared tissue from inside a **68-MILLION-YEAR-OLD** *T. rex* **bone** to **21 LIVING ANIMALS** and found the creatures with the **MOST SIMILAR** proteins were **CHICKENS** and **OSTRICHES.**

The **ostrich** is the **LARGEST BIRD** in the **WORLD TODAY** at **9 FT** (2.7m) **TALL.**

Pelicans have **MOUTH POUCHES** that can hold **3 TIMES** more fish than their stomachs can.

The ostrich is the **WORLD'S FASTEST-RUNNING BIRD**, able to sprint at **43MPH** (69kph). It is thought that *Ornithomimus* could reach similar **SPEEDS**.

Each inner toe on a **CASSOWARY'S** foot has a **SHARP CLAW** up to **5IN** (13cm) long–it slices with them just like **THERIZINOSAURUS** did.

The **5FT 6IN-** (1.7m-) tall **CASSOWARY** amplifies calls through a casque on its head. That's similar to the **HELMETLIKE** structure of *Corythoraptor.*

The **CASQUE** on the **PREHISTORIC-LOOKING HELMETED HORNBILL'S BEAK** can be up to **10%** **OF ITS TOTAL BODY WEIGHT.**

At **2½IN** (6cm) long, the **bee hummingbird** is the **WORLD'S SMALLEST BIRD–** and also the **SMALLEST-EVER DINOSAUR.**

A **shoebill** has a **HOOKED BEAK** up to **10IN** (25cm) **LONG,** strong enough to **CRUSH A BABY CROCODILE.**

With a **WINGSPAN** of up to **4FT** (1.2m), the **RED-LEGGED SERIEMA CAN FLY** but prefers to **ROAM ON THE GROUND,** killing prey by **BEATING IT AGAINST ROCKS.**

GLOSSARY

Amber
Fossilized tree resin. Organisms can be preserved within it.

Amphibian
A cold-blooded vertebrate that can live both on land and in water. Examples include frogs and newts.

Ancestor
An early type of animal or plant from which modern species have developed.

Archosaur
Any of a large group of reptiles that emerged during the Triassic Period. Archosaurs include all crocodiles, birds, dinosaurs, and pterosaurs.

Arthropod
An animal with no spine, jointed legs, a segmented body, and a hard outer skin, like a shell. Examples include scorpions, crabs, and millipedes.

Aquatic
Living in or related to water. "Semiaquatic" animals spend part of their lives in water.

Avian dinosaur
A bird. Modern birds are considered to be avian dinosaurs as they are the last surviving members of a group of two-legged dinosaurs called theropods.

Biota
The animal and plant life found at a specific time and place.

Cambrian
The first geologic period of the Paleozoic Era. The Cambrian lasted from around 542 to 485 million years ago and is when many major animal groups start to appear in the fossil record.

Caniform
Any doglike carnivore of the mammal group Caniformia. Examples include bears, wolves, and foxes.

Carapace
A hard, protective covering or shell on the back of animals, such as crustaceans and turtles.

Carboniferous
A period of the Late Paleozoic Era. Lasting from around 359 to 299 million years ago, it was a time of large invertebrates and diverse amphibians.

Carnivore
An animal that eats other animals.

Cartilage
A tough, rubbery tissue found in the skeletons of vertebrates. Some fish, such as sharks, have skeletons that are entirely made of cartilage.

Cretaceous
The last geologic period of the Mesozoic Era. The Cretaceous lasted from around 145 to 66 million years ago and ended with the extinction of all nonavian dinosaurs.

Cycad
A palmlike plant with fernlike leaves.

Denticle
A small tooth or toothlike projection on an animal's body, often found on skin or exoskeletons.

Descendant
A person, plant, or animal that is directly related to an individual or species from an earlier time.

Devonian Period
A geologic period of the Paleozoic Era. The Devonian Period lasted from around 419 to 359 million years ago and is characterized by the many new species of fish that developed in the Devonian seas.

Digit
A finger or toe.

Dinosaur
Any member of a group of mostly extinct reptiles with upright limbs that were the dominant life form on Earth for over 140 million years during the Mesozoic Era.

DNA
A complex molecule that contains instructions for development, growth, and reproduction. All living organisms have DNA within their cells.

Echinoderm
A marine invertebrate with a hard outer covering that is often spiny. Modern examples, such as starfish and sea urchins, have five-rayed symmetry.

Embryo
An animal or plant that is in an early stage of development, growing from an egg or a seed.

Environment
The surroundings or conditions in which people, animals, and plants live. It includes air, water, and land, and other living and nonliving things.

Era
A distinct, very long span of time covering hundreds of millions of years of Earth's history. Each era is divided into periods. For instance, the Mesozoic Era is divided into the Triassic, Jurassic, and Cretaceous Periods.

Evolution
The gradual development in the characteristics of a species over many years as they adapt to changes in their environment.

Excavation
The act of digging in the ground or removing earth to uncover things, such as fossils.

Exoskeleton
The hard outer covering found on many invertebrates.

Extinct
A species that no longer exists and has no living members.

Femur
The long thighbone in the upper part of the leg. Generally it is the longest bone in an animal's skeleton.

Fish
A cold-blooded animal that lives wholly in water, breathes through gills, and mostly lacks limbs with digits. Examples include salmon, seahorses, and sharks.

Flipper
A wide, flat limb that is used for swimming by various animals.

Forelimb
A front limb of an animal, such as a foreleg, wing, or arm.

Formation
A distinctive layer of rock.

Fossil
The remains or traces of a prehistoric organism preserved in rock, providing physical evidence of former life.

Gene
An instruction within DNA that encodes a particular function or trait, such as eye colour. Parents pass genes on to their offspring.

Habitat
The natural environment where an organism lives and grows, such as the desert or the ocean.

Herbivore
An animal that feeds on plants.

Hindlimb
A back limb of an animal.

Imprint fossil
The preserved impression of a plant or animal in rock. These fossils don't contain any organic material.

Invertebrate
An animal without a spine (backbone). Invertebrates, such as insects and mollusks, account for the majority of animal species.

Jurassic
The second geologic period of the Mesozoic Era. The Jurassic Period lasted from around 201 to 145 million years ago.

K-Pg Extinction
A mass extinction caused by an asteroid hitting Earth that wiped out nonavian dinosaurs around 66 million years ago.

It marks the boundary between the Cretaceous and Paleogene Periods, as well as between the Mesozoic and Cenozoic Eras.

Mammal
Any warm-blooded vertebrate that gives birth to live young and feeds its offspring with milk. Examples include cats, deer, and humans.

Marine
Related to or found in saltwater environments, such as oceans and seas.

Marine reptile
A reptile that has adapted to life in a marine environment. Examples include ichthyosaurs, plesiosaurs, and sea turtles.

Marsupial
Any mammal that carries their young in a pouch on the mother's belly. Examples include opossums and kangaroos.

Mass extinction
A period of time in which a high percentage (usually defined as about 75%) of species go extinct.

Mesozoic
The second of Earth's three major geologic eras. The Mesozoic lasted from around 251 to 66 million years ago and is characterized by the appearance and disappearance of dinosaurs.

Miocene
The first geologic epoch of the Neogene Period, marked by warm climates. The Miocene Epoch lasted from around 23 to 5.3 million years ago.

Neogene
A geologic period of time that lasted from around 23 to 2.5 million years ago. The Neogene Period consists of the Miocene and Pliocene Epochs.

Newton
The standard unit of measurement used to describe force. One Newton is equal to the force it would take to move an object weighing one kilogram one meter per second squared.

Nonavian dinosaur
Any dinosaur that is not a bird. They are all long extinct, with the last dying out

during the K-Pg Extinction around 66 million years ago.

Omnivore
An organism that eats both plants and animals.

Oospecies
An ootaxon (eggshell type), equivalent to a species, used to classify fossilized dinosaur eggs.

Osteoderm
A bony deposit, in the form of a scale, plate, or other structure, in the skin of an animal.

Paleogene
The first period in the Cenozoic Era. The Paleogene Period lasted from around 66 to 23 million years ago and is when modern mammals started to develop.

Paleontologist
A scientist studying the fossils of animals and plants.

Paleontology
The scientific study of ancient life, especially through fossils.

Period
A long span of time lasting millions of years that is often defined by the rock

layers formed over that period. The Triassic is a period.

Permian
A period lasting from around 299 to 252 million years ago. It ended with a mass extinction that wiped out almost all animal species.

Pleistocene
The epoch when modern humans first appeared. It occurred between around 2.5 million years ago and 11,700 years ago.

Precambrian
A vast span of time that began at Earth's formation 4.6 billion years ago and lasted right up to the start of the Cambrian Period 542 million years ago. For most of the era, the only life forms were single-celled and microscopic.

Predator
An animal that hunts and kills other animals for food.

Prey
An animal that is hunted and killed for food by a predator.

Primate
A member of the mammal group with

grasping hands and large brains that includes humans, lemurs, and monkeys.

Primitive
At an early stage of evolution.

Protomammal
Also known as an early synapsid, an ancestor of mammals. Protomammals ruled the land during the Late Paleozoic and Early Mesozoic Eras.

Pterosaur
An extinct type of flying reptile that lived during the Mesozoic Era alongside dinosaurs.

Reptile
A cold-blooded vertebrate, such as a lizard or snake, that is covered in scales or bony plates. Reptiles mostly live on land and lay eggs to reproduce.

Rodent
Any of a large group of mainly small mammals, including mice and rats, that have continuously growing incisor teeth.

Sauropod
Any of a group of four-legged, plant-eating dinosaurs

that included the largest animals to walk Earth.

Scute
A protective bony plate under the skin or shell of a reptile.

Skull
The bones that make up the structure of an animal's head and protect its brain.

Species
A type of plant or animal. Individuals that make up the species can breed with one another to produce offspring that can also reproduce.

Specimen
A sample from an individual animal or plant that is examined or displayed as an example of their species.

Supercontinent
A landmass containing two or more major continental plates. Prehistoric examples from the time of the dinosaurs include Pangea, Laurasia, and Gondwana.

Theropod
Any of a diverse group of mostly carnivorous, two-legged dinosaurs

with grasping hands that had hollow bones and were often three-toed. Examples include *T. rex* and modern birds.

Trace fossil
Fossilized evidence of ancient animals or plants, such as nests, footprints, feces, or burrows.

Triassic
The first period of the Mesozoic, lasting from around 252 to 201 million years ago. Dinosaurs first appeared at the end of the Triassic, and the supercontinent Pangea began to break up.

Vertebra
Any of a series of small, disc-shaped bones in the skeleton that interlock to form the flexible spine or backbone (as well as the neck and tail) of an animal.

Vertebrate
An animal with a spine (backbone).

Wingspan
Maximum length that wings can extend. The wingspan is measured from tip to tip.

PRONUNCIATION GUIDE

Allosaurs: *AL-oh-SORES*
Ammonoids: *am-MUH-noids*
Ankylosaurs: *an-KIE-loh-SORES*
Archaeopteryx: *ar-kee-OP-ter-ix*
Brachiosaurs: *brack-EE-oh-SORES*
Camarasaurids: *KAM-a-ra-SORE-ids*
Caniforms: *cane-ih-FORMS*
Carcharodontosaurs: *CAR-ka-roe-DON-toe-SORES*
Ceratopsians: *serra-TOP-see-uhns*
Ceratosaurs: *see-RAT-oh-SORES*
Chelicerates: *kell-ISS-er-ATES*
Coelophysis: *SEE-low-FYE-sis*
Compsognathids: *COMP-sog-NATH-ids*
Diplodocids: *diplo-DOH-kids*
Dromaeosaurs: *DROH-mee-oh-SORES*
Echinoderms: *ee-KYE-no-derms*
Eoraptor: *EE-oh-RAP-tor*
Fuxianhuia: *fuk-SWEE-on-WEE-ya*
Glyptodonts: *GLIP-toe-donts*
Hadrosaurs: *HAD-roh-SORES*
Herrerasaurids: *heh-RARE-ra-SORE-ids*
Ichthyosaurs: *ICK-thee-oh-SORES*
Iguanodonts: *ig-GWAH-no-donts*
Lambeosaurs: *LAM-bee-oh-SORES*
Mamenchisaurids: *ma-MEN-chee-SORE-ids*
Marsupials: *ma-SOO-pee-uhls*
Mosasaurs: *MOSE-ah-SORES*
Myriapods: *mirr-ee-uh-PODS*
Neotheropods: *NEE-oh-THER-oh-PODS*
Nothosaurs: *NO-tho-SORES*
Ornithomimids: *OR-nith-oh-MY-mids*
Oviraptorosaurs: *oh-VEE-rap-TOH-ruh-SORES*
Pachycephalosaurs: *PACK-ee-SEF-ah-low-SORES*
Placodonts: *PLACK-uh-donts*
Plesiosaurs: *PLEE-see-oh-SORES*
Prosauropods: *pro-SORE-uh-pods*
Psittacosaurs: *si-tak-oh-SORES*
Pterosaurs: *TEH-roe-SORES*
Rauisuchians: *raw-ee-SUCH-ee-uhns*
Spinosaurids: *SPY-noh-SORE-ids*
Stegosaurs: *STEG-oh-SORES*
Therizinosaurs: *THERRY-zin-oh-SORES*
Titanosaurs: *tie-TAN-oh-SORES*
Trilobites: *try-LUH-bites*
Tyrannosaurs: *TIE-ran-oh-SORES*

INDEX

l

Laganosuchus 123
lambeosaurs 130-131
Lambeosaurus 131
lampreys 30, 31
Lariosaurus 50, 51, 61
Laurasia 71
lepidopterans 28
Leptocleididae 87
Leptomeryx 159
Lestodon 178
Limusaurus 74
Liopleurodon 50, 87
Llallawavis scagliai 172
Loganellia 31
Lokotunjailurus 165
Lufengosaurus 59
Lurdusaurus 110
Lusotitan 99
Lystrosaurus 42-43, 46

m

Mcnamaraspis kaprios 33
Macrauchenia 158-159
Macroelongatoolithus 132
Madagascar 172, 173
Magnapaulia 131
Magyarosaurus dacus 139
Mahakala omnogovae 100
Maiasaura 116, 117
Majungasaurus 75
mamenchisaurids 76-77
Mamenchisaurus 76, 77
Mamenchisaurus
    sinocanadorum 77, 78-79
mammals
    first 66-67
    hoofed mammals 158-159
    placental mammals 67
mammoths 180-181
Mammothus exilis 180
Mapusaurus 128-129
Marrella 16-17
marsupials 156-157
Massospondylus 58, 59
Mastodonsaurus 43, 49
Materpiscis attenboroughi 33
Mawsonites spriggi 15
Maximites 25
Megacerops 158, 159
Megaloceros 158, 159

Megalodon 35
Megalonyx 178
Meganeura monyi 29
Megatherium 178
Megazostrodon 66
melanosomes 103
Menoceras 166
Merychippus 159
Mesenosaurus 41
Mesohippus 158
Mesoreodon 158
Mesozoic Era 10-11, 108
methane gas emissions 76
Mexico 124, 131, 178
Miacis 160
Micropachycephalosaurus
    hongtuyanensis 100
Microraptor 103, 120
Microraptor gui 100
microtektites 152
millipedes 28-29
Minmi 127
Miragaia 80
mites 27
Mongolia 100, 118, 143,
    147, 149, 156
Morganucodon 67
Morocco 18, 62, 87, 124
mosasaurs 62, 150-151
Mosasaurus 150-151
Mosasaurus hoffmannii 62
Moschops 41
mosquitoes 29
moths 28
Mourasuchus 122
Myanmar 29
Mylodon 178
myriapods 28-29

n

nautiloids 36
neck frills 135
necks, longest 62, 77, 78-79
Nedoceratops 134
Nemicolopterus crypticus 91
Neoepiblema acreensis 163
Neogene Period 10
neotheropods 72-73
nests 91, 118, 132, 139
Netherlands 62, 151
New Zealand 104, 173
Niger 110, 123, 124
Nimravus brachyops 165
Norway 85

Notharctus 176
nothosaurs 50-51
Nothosaurus 50-51
Nyasasaurus 53
Nyctosaurus 90

o

Olorotitan 117, 131
Omeisaurus 76-77
Onychophora 36
Opabinia 16, 17
Ophiacodon 41
Ordovician Period 10
ornithomimids 140-141
Ornithomimus 140, 141, 183
ornithopods 114, 115
osteoderms 49, 60, 74, 122,
    127
ostriches 182, 183
Otodus megalodon 34
Ottoia 17
Oviraptor 132, 133
oviraptorosaurs 132-133
oxygen, atmospheric 29, 46

p

pachycephalosaurs 142-143
Pachycephalosaurus 142
Pakicetus inachus 170
Palaeocastor 163
Palaeocoma 20
Paleogene Period 10
Palaeoisopus problematicus 26
palaeontologists 6, 9
Palaeopropithecus 176-177
Paleozoic Era 18
Pampadromaeus 52
Pangea 46, 47, 53, 55, 56,
    71, 89
Panphagia 52
Panthera atrox 164
Paraceratherium 166, 167
Parameteoraspis 31
Paramylodon 178
Parapuzosia seppenradensis 24
Parasaurolophus 8, 116-117
Parioscorpio venator 26
Patagotitan 129, 138, 139
pelicans 182
Pelorovis 159
Pentaceratops 134

Permian Period 10, 40, 42
Perucetus colossus 171
phorusrhacids 172-173
Phorusrhacos 172
Pinacosaurus grangeri 126
placoderms 32-33
placodonts 60-61
Placodus 60
Platecarpus 151
Plateosaurus 58-59
plesiosaurs 50, 62, 70,
    86-89
Plesiosaurus dolichodeirus 89
Plesiosaurus macrocephalus
    89
pliosaurs 86-87
Polycotylus latippinus 87
Porifera 36
Portugal 94, 99
possums 156
Postosuchus 48-49
Precambrian 10
Prestosuchus 48
primates 176-177
Prionosuchus plummeri 38
Priscoculex burmanicus 29
Proceratosaurus 146
Procoptodon 156, 157
Protoceratops 135
protomammals 10, 40-41
Protosuchus 123
Psephoderma 60, 61
psittacosaurs 118-119
Psittacosaurus 118-119
Pteranodon 91
Pterodactylus 88, 91
pterosaurs 10, 90-91
    wingspans 144-145
Pterygotus 26-27
Puertasaurus 138
Puijila darwini 161
Pulmonoscorpius kirktonensis
    27
Purgatorius 176, 177
Purussaurus 123, 124

q

Quaternary Period 11
Quetzalcoatlus northropi 90,
    144-145

R

rauisuchians 48–49
red-legged seriema 183
reefs 11, 71
Repenomamus 119
reptiles, early 10, 11
rhinos 158, 166–167, 168
Rhyniognatha hirstii 28
Riparovenator milnerae 112
rodents 162–163
Rolfosteus 32
Romania 144
Russia 15, 18, 41, 118, 131

S

sabre-toothed cats 164–165,
    178
Sacabambaspis 31
Sahelanthropus 177
sails 41, 113
Sanjuansaurus 57
Sarcosuchus 122, 124–125
saurischians 57
sauropodomorphs 52
sauropods 8, 52, 55, 57, 70,
    71, 76–77, 82–83, 92–93,
    114, 115, 138–139
    prosauropods 58–59
Sauroposeidon proteles 78
Saurosuchus 49, 57
scavengers 57, 105, 129
Scipionyx 104
scorpions 26, 27
Scotty (*T. rex* skeleton) 146
scutes 49, 81, 174, 175
"sea dragons" *see* plesiosaurs
sea level rises 108
sea lilies 20
sea scorpions 26, 27
sea spiders 26, 27
Sebecus 122
Seirocrinus 20
sequoia 71
Seymouria 38
Shantungosaurus 116
sharks 34–35
shoebills 183
Shonisaurus sikanniensis
    62–63
Shuangbaisaurus 73
Siberia 42, 167, 180

Silurian Period 11
Simosuchus 123
single-celled organisms 10
Sinocalliopteryx 104
Sinocephale bexelli 143
Sinoconodon 66–67
Sinornithosaurus 103, 120
Sinosauropteryx 102, 104,
    105
Sinosaurus triassicus 72
sloths 178–179
Smilodon 164, 165
sounds 130, 158
South Africa 165
Spain 18, 114–115
speeds 9, 64, 73, 74, 84, 91,
    94, 103, 111, 115, 117,
    119, 121, 128, 131, 133,
    140, 172, 183
Spicomellus afer 126
spiders 26, 27
spinosaurids 112–113, 114
Spinosaurus 7, 112–113, 128
sponges 16, 36, 71
Spriggina 14
Squaloraja 88
squid 24, 85
Staurikosaurus 57
stegosaurs 70, 71, 80–81
Stegosaurus 80–81, 95
Stenopterygius 84–85
Stethacanthus 35
Suchomimus 113
supercontinents 46, 47, 71
Supersaurus vivianae 78
Swarpuntia 15

T

Tachiraptor 73
tail clubs 77, 126, 175
tail spikes 80, 175
Tanzania 75, 76, 81, 98, 177
Tarbosaurus 147
Teleoceras 166, 167, 168–
    169
Teleoceras major 169
teleosts 47
Temnodontosaurus 84
Temnospondyls 43
temperatures 42, 46, 70,
    108
Tentosaurus 110, 111
terror birds 172–173
Tethys Sea 46, 71

thagomizer 80
Thailand 118
Thanatosdrakon amaru 144
Thecodontosaurus 58
therizinosaurs 148–149
Therizinosaurus 148–149,
    183
theropods 7, 49, 52, 57,
    74–75, 94–95, 104–105,
    114, 115, 140–141,
    148–149, 182
    neotheropods 72–73
thumb spikes 110, 111
Thylacoleo 156, 157
Tianyuraptor 102
ticks 26, 27
timeline 10–11
Titanichthys 32
Titanis 172, 173
titanosaurs 78, 109, 138–139
Torosaurus 135
trees 46, 70, 71, 109
Triasacarus fedelei 27
Triassic Period 10, 44–67
Tribrachidium heraldicum 14
Triceratops 100, 134, 135,
    136–137
Trigonotarbida 27
trilobites 10, 18–19, 43
Trinucleus 19
Tunisia 124
tusks 124, 180, 181
Tutcetus rayanensis 171
Tylosaurus 151
tyrannosaurids 122
tyrannosaurs 103, 123,
    146–147
Tyrannosaurus rex 7, 52, 75,
    146–147, 182
Tyrannotitan 128, 129

U

Uintatherium 159
ungulates (hoofed mammals)
    158–159
United Kingdom 15, 20, 27,
    28, 80, 86, 88–89, 111,
    112
US 34, 41, 62, 64, 73, 78, 83,
    87, 100, 120, 124, 134,
    136–137, 144, 149, 165,
    166, 167, 168–169, 178
Utahraptor 120, 121

V

Vegavis 109
Velociraptor 120, 121, 182
velvet worms 36
Venezuela 73, 124
vertebrates, earliest 16
volcanic eruptions 42, 102,
    153, 168–169
vomit 85
Vorombe titan 173

W

Walliserops 19
Wamweracaudia 76
Wellnhoferia 96
whales 170–171
Wiwaxia 16
wolves 161, 178
wombats 156
woodmice 163
woolly mammoths 180–181

X

Xenosmilus hodsonae 165
Xinjiangtitan 78
xiphosurans 27

Y

young
    care of the 48, 116, 118
    live birth 33, 67, 87, 150,
    157
Yutyrannus 102, 108–109, 147

Z

Zalambdalestes 66
Zhengyuanlong 102
Zuniceratops 134

ACKNOWLEDGMENTS

The publisher would like to thank the following people for their help in the making of this book:
Marie Lorimer for the index; Nick Funnell for proofreading; Claire Lister and Danni Turner for editing; Andrew Fishleigh, Terry Sambridge, Matthew Taylor, Annie Arnold, Kerry Churcher, and Simon Oliver for design; Suhita Dharamjit and Tanya Mehrotra for jacket design; Dr. Xiaoya Ma and Giquello for kindly supplying images; and Sarah Smithies for picture research.

Picture Credits

The publisher would like to thank the following for their kind permission to reproduce their photographs:

(Key: a-above; b-below/bottom; c-center; f-far; l-left; r-right; t-top)

4 Alamy Stock Photo: Stocktrek Images, Inc. (c). **Shutterstock.com:** Esteban De Armas (tr). **5 Alamy Stock Photo:** Daniel Eskridge (tr). **Getty Images:** Mark Garlick / Science Photo Library (tl). **Shutterstock.com:** Warpaint (c). **6 Dorling Kindersley:** Colin Keates / Natural History Museum, London (br). **7 Alamy Stock Photo:** Science Photo Library (t). **8 Alamy Stock Photo:** Corey Ford (bl). **8-9 Alamy Stock Photo:** Daniel Eskridge. **9 Alamy Stock Photo:** Zoonar GmbH (cr). **Science Photo Library:** Julius T Csotonyi (br). **10 Alamy Stock Photo:** Dotted Zebra (tc); Mark Turner (br). **11 Alamy Stock Photo:** Leonello Calvetti (cr); Stocktrek Images, Inc. (tl). **Dorling Kindersley:** Dreamstime.com: Rixie (br). **Shutterstock.com:** Catmando (tr). **13 Shutterstock.com:** Esteban De Armas. **14-15 Shutterstock.com:** Dotted Yeti. **16-17 Shutterstock.com:** Dotted Yeti. **18-19 Science Photo Library:** Walter Myers. **22 Dr. Xiaoya Ma**. **24-25 Shutterstock.com:** Esteban De Armas. **26-27 Getty Images:** Warpaintcobra. **28-29 Shutterstock.com:** Catmando. **30-31 Alamy Stock Photo:** Stocktrek Images, Inc.. **32 Science Photo Library:** Jose Antonio Peñas. **34-35 Science Photo Library:** JA Chirinos. **36-37 Alamy Stock Photo:** Reinhard Dirscherl.

38-39 Dreamstime.com: Planetfelicity. **40-41 Science Photo Library:** Jose Antonio Peñas. **42-43 Alamy Stock Photo:** Science Photo Library. **45 Alamy Stock Photo:** Stocktrek Images, Inc.. **46-47 Shutterstock.com:** Rodos Studio / Ferhat Cinar. **48-49 Shutterstock.com:** Design Projects (background); Warpaint. **50-51 Shutterstock.com:** Catmando. **52-53 Getty Images:** Buena Vista Images. **54-55 Science Photo Library:** Millard H. Sharp. **56-57 Science Photo Library:** James Kuether. **58-59 Dreamstime.com:** Mr1805. **60-61 Science Photo Library:** JA Chirinos. **62-63 Alamy Stock Photo:** Stocktrek Images, Inc.. **64-65 Dorling Kindersley:** 123RF.com: Michael Rosskothen. **69 Getty Images:** Mark Garlick / Science Photo Library. **70-71 Science Photo Library:** Mark Garlick. **72-73 Alamy Stock Photo:** Daniel Eskridge. **74-75 Dreamstime.com:** Mr1805. **76-77 Alamy Stock Photo:** MasPix. **78-79 Shutterstock.com:** Elenarts. **80-81 Getty Images:** Elena Duvernay / Stocktrek Images. **82-83 Dreamstime.com:** Mr1805. **84-85 Dreamstime.com:** Planetfelicity. **86-87 Shutterstock.com:** Warpaint. **88-89 Science Photo Library:** Natural History Museum, London. **90-91 Shutterstock.com:** Daniel Eskridge. **92-93 Shutterstock.com:** Michael Rosskothen. **94-95 Alamy Stock Photo:** MasPix. **96-97 Shutterstock.com:** Daniel Eskridge. **98-99 Getty Images:** Mark Garlick / Science Photo Library. **100-101 Science Photo Library:** Julius T Csotonyi. **102-103 Science Photo Library:** Martin Shields. **104-105 Shutterstock.com:** Dotted Yeti. **107 Shutterstock.com:** Herschel Hoffmeyer (background); Warpaint. **108-109 Science Photo Library:** James Kuether. **110-111 Getty Images:** Elena Duvernay / Stocktrek Images. **112-113 Alamy Stock Photo:** Stocktrek Images, Inc.. **114-115 Alamy Stock Photo:** Jos Mara Barres Manuel. **116-117 Dreamstime.com:** Daniel Eskridge. **118-119 Bob Nicholls:** (c). **Shutterstock.com:** Herschel Hoffmeyer (background). **120-121 Alamy Stock Photo:** Science Photo Library. **122-123 Alamy Stock**

Photo: Michael Rosskothen. **124-125 Science Photo Library:** JA Chirinos. **126-127 Shutterstock.com:** Daniel Eskridge. **128-129 Getty Images:** MR1805. **130-131 Dreamstime.com:** Mr1805. **132-133 Alamy Stock Photo:** Stocktrek Images, Inc.. **134-135 Shutterstock.com:** Herschel Hoffmeyer (background); Warpaint. **136-137 Giquello**. **138-139 Alamy Stock Photo:** Dotted Zebra. **140-141 Alamy Stock Photo:** Science Photo Library. **142-143 Shutterstock.com:** Daniel Eskridge. **144-145 Alamy Stock Photo:** MasPix. **146-147 Dorling Kindersley:** 123rf.com: Leonello Calvetti. **Shutterstock.com:** Herschel Hoffmeyer (background). **148-149 Science Photo Library:** Jose Antonio Peñas. **150-151 Dorling Kindersley:** Dreamstime.com: Planetfelicity. **152-153 Alamy Stock Photo:** Science Photo Library. **155 Alamy Stock Photo:** Daniel Eskridge. **156-157 Roman Uchytel**. **158-159 Dorling Kindersley:** Dreamstime.com: Ralf Kraft. **160-161 Roman Uchytel**. **164-165 Alamy Stock Photo:** Daniel Eskridge. **166-167 Dreamstime.com:** Mr1805. **168-169 Alamy Stock Photo:** Archive PL. **170-171 Science Photo Library:** Roman Uchytel. **172-173 Getty Images:** Sergey Krasovskiy. **174-175 Alamy Stock Photo:** Stocktrek Images, Inc.. **176-177 Roman Uchytel**. **178-179 Roman Uchytel**. **180-181 Dreamstime.com:** Junichi Shimazaki. **182-183 Shutterstock.com:** Wirestock Creators.

All other images © Dorling Kindersley

our WORLD in NUMBERS

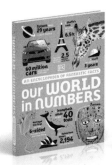 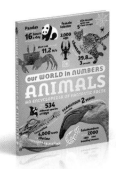 

our WORLD in PICTURES

   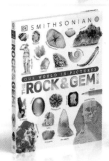 

FLASH CARDS

    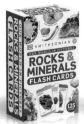